"Kathryn just gets it. As a mentor and coach, she validated my worldview but also challenged me to not stay there exclusively—she pushed me to grow. Her approach is inspirational but also simple, tactical and actionable. Her lessons are worth heeding. They've proved invaluable to me over the years."

—*Corrie Heck Scott, Director Global Communications for Food & Water Sustainability, The Nature Conservancy*

"This is truly one of the most inspiring pieces I have ever read."

—*Lauren Carroll, Executive Director, Sexual Assault Resource Center*

"Kathryn is the true definition of a mentor and I am so glad to call her one of mine! I had the privilege of working for and with Kathryn a few times throughout my career. She is a tremendous leader and really challenges you to look at the bigger picture and not sweat the small stuff. So read her book, absorb her stories and you will be learning from the best...simply put, the very best."

—*Megan Parsons, VP Human Resources, The Libman Company*

"I truly believe that leaders and their teams will benefit so much from this book. The personal stories are important and impactful. The fact that Kathryn started off raw and became the fabulous leader and mentor she is today will encourage others to reach. Leaders don't always start off strong. It takes work and Kathryn shows how to do the work through her stories. Priceless!"

—*Linda Kraftzenk, former Director of Corporate Communications, Caterpillar*

"I just finished this book and I loved it! It has some amazing information in it! I loved the personal stories and the experiences. I took away some pearls for sure. Acknowledging and embracing generational differences in the workplace is essential for any leader. The millennial generation is steeped with talent and enthusiasm that if provided the right environment can lead our organizations into a brighter future. Kathryn's expertise and experience with leadership and mentoring millennials helps bring understanding to their differences as well as ignites curiosity to want to cultivate this next generation and step out of their way to see just how far they can go!"

—*Anne Schutt, Financial Advisor, Waite Financial Group, Northwestern Mutual*

"*Rock Star Millennials* didn't just encourage the 'work hard play hard' mentality that I already had, it gave me tools and action items in **speed mode** to mold me into the person and leader I am striving to be. Here's your action item: Read the book and learn from one of the best."

—*Amber Kienast, Marketing Manager, Renewal by Andersen of Central Illinois and Quad Cities*

D1065545

"I thoroughly enjoyed reading this. I learned some things and was reminded of other topics/tools I haven't used in a while. Thanks for that teaching Kathryn!"

—Jackie McBrady, Sr. Director, Lead-Finance Applications EMEA, Cushman & Wakefield

"I cannot thank Kathryn enough for the guidance and shift in mindset that not only has improved my professional life but my personal life as well!"

—Kelsey Meek, Business Manager, Renewal by Andersen of Central Illinois and Quad Cities

"*Rock Star Millennials* is truly the culmination of Kathryn's career as a servant leader. Her candidness brings to life simple yet highly effective tools proven to 'develop people for life.' In sharing her toolbox, Kathryn is continuing the legacy of her leader, proving that mentoring is contagious."

— Diane Shankwitz, retired Fortune 50 corporate communicator and breast cancer mentor

"The practices Kathryn taught me continue to enable my success. The nature of work continues to change, and women must learn tools and techniques to enable their own success. Kathryn's powerful example of servant-leadership will inspire many and this book will serve as a resource to enable professional success for many Rock Star Millennials to come."

—Kathryn Reilly , Senior Vice President, Aon

"Eye opening, to me, that *Rock Star Millennials* are looking for the same things I wanted when I started working 40+ years ago. I had lost sight of that! Thank you for reminding me."

—Lynn Reinacher, Group Manager, Office Site Services and Accounting, Nestlé Purina Pet Care

"I still use the 90-Day Log (3-Bucket Exercise) I learned at Caterpillar to onboard new employees. It helps us be super transparent about what's working and what's not. I also remember what Kathryn taught me when I went to Little Rock for my first job. She said, 'Whether they're in the office or in the factory, get to know your people.'"

—Adam Hamilton, Director of Digital and Social, McDonald's

"The best way to describe this book is that it's truly a gift...it's like taking decades of the best personal and professional advice on mentoring and leadership and wrapping it up in the most simple and beautiful package so you can share it with others. There are very few things that feel as good as seeing a young person grow and gain confidence in themselves. This book uses engaging stories to give a practical guide to developing people for life."

—Marcy Wiegardt, Global Marketing & Segment Talent Manager, Caterpillar

ROCK STAR
MILLENNIALS

DEVELOPING THE
NEXT GENERATION
OF LEADERS

KATHRYN D. SPITZNAGLE

MENTORING WOMEN MILLENIALS

Rock Star Millennials: Developing the Next Generation of Leaders

Published by:
Mentoring Women Millennials, LLC, Edwards, IL 61528
www.mentoringwomenmillennials.com

Project Managed by:
Write Along With You, LLC, Peachtree City, GA 30269

Ordering Information:
Quantity sales. Special discounts are available on quantity purchases by corporations, associations, and others. For details, contact the publisher at the address above.

ISBN: 978-1-7360836-0-4 (HB)
ISBN: 978-1-7360836-1-1 (Trade Paperback)
ISBN: 978-1-7360836-2-8 (eBook)
ISBN: 978-1-7360836-3-5 (Audiobook)
ISBN: 978-1-7360836-4-2 (Digital PDF of Leadership Tools)
ISBN: 978-1-7360836-5-9 (Bound Leadership Tools)

Library of Congress Control Number: 2020922566

All photos in this work with people are used with their permission.

Printed in USA

First Edition

14 13 12 11 10 / 10 9 8 7 6 5 4 3 2 1

Cover Design and Interior Formatting by Becky's Graphic Design, LLC

This book was written to honor the seasoned leaders who invested in me, to encourage the developing leaders who are honing their craft and to inspire tomorrow's leaders to continue the legacy.

In this book, I am sharing my journey to becoming a leader of millennials so I could help you with yours.

CONTENTS

FOREWORD

IN THE FIRST QUARTER OF 2004, my phone rang. My colleague, Kathryn Spitznagle, was calling to congratulate me on my recently-announced promotion. I knew Kathryn a bit through projects at our company but not personally. What I did know was: she was senior to me professionally, always impeccably dressed and very engaging personally.

At the time, I was relocating to Washington, DC to work on corporate public policy issues. The opportunity was simultaneously exciting and intimidating. While I was thrilled about the interesting professional challenge, I was apprehensive about moving cross country on my own and to be the only professional woman working in the office. Kathryn explained that we might speak regularly to strategize about opportunities and obstacles that I encountered in my new adventure.

I was touched at her thoughtful outreach to share her personal well-wishes as well as intrigued at her invitation to engage in a mentoring project with her. As we chatted, I learned that she and I shared the same alma matter. She had worked in New York and St. Louis, and her previous work took her abroad frequently. I took a risk and accepted the offer. I thought I might pick up a thing or two along the way.

In hindsight, I am most grateful for the lessons I learned working with Kathryn. First, she encouraged me to adopt visualization as a method to realize success. Prior to my relocation, she casually suggested that I might look for opportunities to explore Washington from afar and imagine myself there. I watched The West Wing, The American President and Broadcast News. And while I had visited Washington frequently for business, I found the viewing experience immersive as I envisioned myself there. Later this exercise was oddly validating. I frequently took meetings in the office building at 1001 Pennsylvania Avenue, NW (where Broadcast News was filmed) and the Eisenhower Executive Office Building (where I half-expected Josh Lyman to walk through at any moment). And while there, I felt capable and self-assured. I was excited to be working in notable places with decision makers and conducted my business with a sense of focus and purpose, rather than driven to distraction by historic places and imposing settings.

In addition to visualizing my success, Kathryn guided me in the practice of conducting a weekly review. Each Friday, I would analyze the week's happenings and evaluate what went well and what could be improved. The habit allowed me to reflect on the days and weeks that unfolded so quickly. This process also allowed me to review events objectively and articulate my feelings about what transpired. By celebrating successes and strategizing about how best to overcome failures, I had the confidence to tackle new, more interesting and more challenging projects. This weekly review enabled me to accomplish some of my most fulfilling professional accomplishments including: leading coalitions of my counterparts on public policy issues which resulted in the enactment of significant health and retirement laws, planning events to celebrate the inaugurations of two incoming presidents and earning my MBA at Georgetown.

I spent six years in Washington—it was a dynamic and fascinating time. I now have more than two decades of work experience and the lessons I learned early on have served me well. As my career continues to change and evolve —due to new professional projects and opportunities, international business travel, more recent demands of "remote" work, as well as balancing my professional goals with wonderful developments in my personal life—the practices Kathryn taught me continue to enable my success. The nature of work continues to change, and women must learn tools and techniques to enable their own success. Kathryn's powerful example of servant-leadership will inspire many and this book will serve as a resource to enable professional success for many Rock Star Millennials to come.

Kathryn Reilly
Senior Vice President, Aon

INTRODUCTION

WHEN I SHARE THE NAME OF my company, Mentoring Women Millennials, the response I often get from other leaders is, "Good. They need it," along with a story about a young person they're struggling to lead. The more speaking I did, the more I got this same response and understood not only is there a need to mentor millennials, there's a need to train leaders on different ways to coach and develop this generation. Why is that important? It is estimated that by 2025, 75% of the workforce will be millennials. So, if you're a leader who is interested in attracting, retaining and developing future leaders, these are your employees and now is the time to engage them.

Who are millennials? Generally speaking, anyone born between 1980 and the early 2000s is a millennial. For those who work with millennials, you may be asking, how do we best engage, motivate, and inspire them? Or is that our job? I've heard it said that millennials are lazy and entitled. Like any generation, there are certainly instances where these generalizations are true. My experience with millennials is that they are actually one of the hardest working and most creative generations I've worked with throughout the years because they have a "work hard, play hard mentality," they are entrepreneurial and they're always connected because of current technology.

What's your view? To gain a little more insight, let's begin by asking a few questions. When you think of millennials, what words come to mind? Do you see them as creative or as folks who just won't follow the rules? Do you see them as entrepreneurial or as employees who are more focused on re-inventing the wheel than getting the work done? Do you see them as people who want to learn and grow and be inspired or as ones who want to take what the company has to offer, better themselves and then move on? Your answers to these questions will provide some insight into your perceptions and attitudes toward this generation, and your experiences will give us a place to start.

Let's get a little more specific. What do you want from millennials as a boss? What do you want from millennials as a company? What do you want from millennials in terms of leadership and learning? Answers to these questions that I frequently hear are: As a boss, I want millennials to be respectful. I want millennials to show up and come to work. I want millennials to work while they're at work. I want millennials to be part of a team as opposed to a collection of individuals working independently.

So let's take a look at what millennials want. What do they want from a boss? What do they want from a company? And what do they want in terms of leadership and learning? Understanding what they want and how to deliver it in a way that appeals to them is key to engaging and empowering this creative, high-energy, entrepreneurial generation.

As a company founder, and 30-year leader in corporate America, I want millennials to engage, be advocates and demonstrate some loyalty by staying with the company for more than just a few months or a year. In terms of leadership and learning, I want millennials to listen to those with experience and consider their ideas in addition to sharing their own. I want millennials to value learning opportunities that their leaders see will help them grow in addition to learning opportunities that are of interest to them. I want to see millennials appreciate the investment being made in them and in turn give back to others.

In this book, I'll help you take a closer look at both sides of this exchange between leaders and millennials to see how both sides can benefit. We'll discuss how we can best serve millennials as their leaders and mentors, and in return, how can they best serve us as team members, engaged employees and future leaders. You'll see many real-life examples from a variety of companies including Nestlé-Purina, Caterpillar Inc., Renewal by Andersen, McDonald's and some smaller firms as well. I've added these to illustrate true leadership in action and provide ideas to apply in your workplace.

Most of my corporate colleagues have years of experience understanding their industries, their companies and their careers. They also know what they want out of their millennial workforce. By sheer time in the workplace, millennials have not yet gained that knowledge, experience or advantage. With that in mind, we'll focus our quest on learning more about them which in turn will help us as leaders target our efforts to be the most successful and productive.

Together, we'll pursue what millennials want from their bosses, from their companies, and from their leadership and learning opportunities. These are the categories that surface regardless of size, industry, or maturity of company. We'll be starting off most sections with a request from a millennial, as if they are speaking to us. (And speaking of "they," please note we've used the plural forms of they, them, their and theirs instead of his/hers to be more inclusive).

As leaders, the teams we lead are more than likely inherited. It's rare that we get to build an entire team of our own choosing. What we do get to choose is how we will lead the team we have, whether chosen or inherited or a combination of both. Through our leadership style, we also get to choose how successful we will be with that team. My purpose in writing this book is to be a conduit, providing you with insights from a converted "Lousy Leader," lessons learned from the many good leaders who invested in grooming me, and the tools acquired along the way. My intent is to introduce a concept, illustrate it with a story, and enable you to initiate action with talking points, a tool, or a process. After all, we both want the same thing—and that's for you to be successful. Let's get started.

Kathryn Spitznagle

PART I

WHAT MILLENNIALS WANT FROM THEIR BOSSES

THE TOP REQUESTS

AS A LEADER, YOU MAY be struggling with how best to recruit, engage and retain millennials. The truth is, what they want from us is not all that different than what we wanted from our leaders. They want flexibility, clear direction, honest feedback, genuine recognition and leadership development. They also want competitive compensation and a clear line of sight to the next level or a plan to get there. One difference with this generation is they know what they want, and they ask for it. They're also looking for a more collaborative relationship with their boss and co-workers. In my experience, a successful leadership style for this generation can be as simple as prioritizing a few key elements or delivering messages in a little different way.

Knowing what they want and need can help you to modify your behavior for optimum relationships and increased engagement which leads to higher productivity and better results. Together, we'll pursue what millennials want from their bosses, from their companies and from their leadership and learning opportunities.

As I mentor and coach millennials, their requests are very specific and consistent, across the country and across industries. Building trust is important to them; developing a personal relationship with their boss is also important to them. They want to know their boss as a person, beyond the job, and they want their boss to know them as a person, beyond the job. Once there's a foundation of trust, they want transparency and support. It really boils down to five simple things:

1. Help me navigate my career.

2. Give me straight feedback.

3. Mentor and coach me.

4. Sponsor me for formal development.

5. Be comfortable with flexible schedules.

Each of these has a dedicated chapter in this book. Now let's look at each one and identify some actionable items that you can take as leaders.

CHAPTER 1

HELP ME NAVIGATE MY CAREER

MOST MILLENNIALS HAVE NEVER BEEN EXPOSED to an evaluation of their skills, much less the idea of a career path or career development. As their leaders, you'll need to help them identify the skills that they have and the ones that need to be developed for their current job and future jobs. To help you, we can talk about three specific needs which have surfaced in my years of training and mentoring:

- Talk to me about transferable skills.
- Identify possible positions where my skills could be best utilized.
- Help me determine if I am a leader or an individual contributor.

TALK TO ME ABOUT TRANSFERABLE SKILLS

Transferable skills are simply skills that can be transferred from one job or position to another. Examples might be communication, collaboration or project management skills. The skills could be applied to any number of jobs throughout someone's career. We often see employees identifying a very literal skill set like writing or editing or public speaking. These literal skills may be components of larger leadership skills, which are also are transferable from one position to another. Likewise, when a position becomes available with literal skills the employee might not possess, they may not even consider applying for a position that could provide an outstanding growth opportunity. We see a gender difference here. Men will look at the skills requirements for a job posting and if they possess a fraction of the skills, they will apply for the job. I've even had men say to me, "Why would you take a job where there isn't room to grow?" Women, on the other hand, will view the same posting and if they possess the majority of the skills but not ALL, they will deem themselves not qualified and not apply. This is where leaders can help truly identify their skills and provide a "nudge" if the employee is reticent to consider an opportunity.

Here's an example. When I worked at Caterpillar, I was a young mom and responsible for leading a corporate media team. I was given the opportunity to build a new facility, the Caterpillar Visitors Center. When I was offered this position I immediately confessed and explained why I wasn't qualified (another thing women frequently do that men do not). I said, "I've never built anything before—not even a house—and this is a $37 million-dollar project. I'm also not an engineer or an architect." My boss saw beyond the literal skills of engineering and architecture and identified the transferable skills he was looking for when he responded, "This project has been in the works for 8 years, and we haven't broken ground. We are currently millions of dollars over budget and thousands of square feet over footprint. I don't need an engineer or an architect. I need a communicator, a collaborator and a project manager," to which I responded happily, "I'm your gal!" and took on the project. Thank goodness for that leader who identified and sought out the transferable skills and then helped me see them as well.

Fast forward a couple years, and we did indeed break ground, after we got the project back on track. I worked with an amazing team of Caterpillar architects and engineers who led us through a "value-engineering" exercise where we ultimately "flipped" the direction of the building and reduced the amenities and actual size of the building to work within the original footprint . As a team, we delivered the project on time and under budget, for which the project won a Chairman's Award—a proud moment indeed.

Another example is from a leader I had at Purina early in my career. He asked me to identify my top three skills and I responded with "writing, editing and public speaking." He was the first one to teach me about the difference between "transactional and transferable skills." He identified writing, editing and public speaking as "transactional skills." These are skills to transact with others and are skills many people possess. They are typically taught in school at some level. He explained these skills would serve me well early in my career and would be building blocks for other leadership skills. "Transferable skills" he said were higher level skills that could serve me well as I continued in leadership and took on other developmental assignments that would take me out of my functional areas of expertise in marketing and communications.

My boss said it this way, "From where I sit, your top three skills are: You have an eye for potential, a head for business, and a heart for people...and I need to see you bring those three skills with you – strong, every day." Today, you might utilize a tool like Gallup's StrengthsFinder™ to identify an employee's transferable skills or "Superpowers." Regardless of what of you call them, identifying these skills and letting your employee know what you see is key.

As a reminder to me he would often hold up three fingers and smile as he walked by my office, and I knew exactly what that meant. He was reminding me of the skills he saw in me and encouraging me to bring them to work "strong, every day." He also had a knack for demonstrating his encouragement, even when I thought he wasn't looking.

One morning I walked past a group of high-level leaders having a focused discussion in the hallway. It looked like the "meeting after the meeting" and sounded a little intense. My leader had his back turned to me, so I was certain he hadn't seen me. I walked behind the group and went on to refill my water bottle at a nearby drinking fountain. When I had gotten my water, I looked down the hall and saw that my leader was holding up three fingers behind his back, and I had to laugh. He was still totally engaged in the discussion, had not made eye contact with me, and yet his communication was clear. Not only had he seen me, he wanted to engage and inspire me at every opportunity. His leadership encouraged me to be my very best self that day—without even saying a word.

IDENTIFY POSSIBLE POSITIONS WHERE MY SKILLS COULD BEST BE UTILIZED

This takes the idea of transferable skills one step further. Once you've helped an employee identify their transactional and transferable skills, help them see how those skills can be utilized in ways that can broaden their career. For example, my leader at Purina encouraged me to do more and more public speaking inside and outside of work...and here's why. He saw that skill as a bridge to other opportunities for me. He said that people often equated good speaking skills with good leadership skills. While he cautioned me to "never confuse a good orator with a good leader," he did say public speaking was a part of inspirational leadership and should be a "well-honed tool in my toolbox."

As he helped me develop the skill through lots of practice and critique – as well as recognition and encouragement – he also gave me the confidence to step outside of my functional area and helped me broaden my career. Remember when we talked earlier about utilizing my skills? This is an example where our conversations led me to explore positions in Public Affairs, Media, Training, Visitor Services, and even Sustainability, all of which had public speaking components, and none of which I would have considered for that reason earlier in my career. Kudos to that leader who helped me see where my transferrable skills could be applied and helped me develop the public speaking skill set, I needed to make me a viable candidate when positions became available.

Not only does this conversation with employees open their eyes to different positions and the corresponding skills, it communicates that you as a leader know them...see potential in them...and value them enough to have the conversation. That in itself is tremendously engaging to this generation and can help build their loyalty as well as leadership within them.

HELP ME DETERMINE IF I AM A LEADER OR AN INDIVIDUAL CONTRIBUTOR

This is a simple conversation that can be pivotal in an employee's career. Not every employee wants to be a leader, but the employee may not see any other way to advance. Or he or she may want to be a leader at some point in their career but know they're not ready yet. Or the employee may have been with the company six months and believe they should be the CEO—yesterday! Because there are so many different perspectives on this, having the conversation with them about where they are and where they want to go can be invaluable.

If they want to be an individual contributor or expert in their craft, help them identify the possible positions or a series of experiences that can help them develop into a well-rounded expert. For example, I worked with an engineer who was very creative and was energized by seeing his ideas become reality and acquiring patents for his inventions. He developed a more broad-based engineering knowledge by working on multiple NPI (New Product Introduction) teams in various capacities throughout his career. He ultimately became a Senior Engineer and although he didn't lead a team, others sought him out for his expertise, and that was rewarding for him. Part of his development plan as an individual contributor was to broaden his expertise within the industry, where he became known as an expert in his field. This created a path for knowledge exchange or benchmarking with others, which brought new ideas to the company and acclaim to him as an expert.

If you have an employee who wants to lead people, help them identify the leadership qualities they've already demonstrated and those that need to be developed. Asking them why they want to be a leader can also provide insight into their purpose. (We'll talk more about the importance of this in Chapter 8.)

For those employees who believe they should have been a leader "yesterday," ask them which role they believe they are qualified for and why. Here's an example. I was working with a non-profit group and mentoring a young employee who had been with them for a few months. He had a passion for the mission and believed he should be a higher-level leader already. His leader was aggravated with his "entitlement" mentality, and the discussion became a source of conflict and confrontation, repeatedly.

I offered the leader an alternative approach. Agree with the employee's premise to get the conversation started, and then probe for "proof of concept." I asked the employee about his fundraising experience and suggested we begin by naming the multi-million-dollar gifts, donations or sponsorships he'd acquired. Then I asked him to describe the relationships that led to those funds and the specific approach he used to make the "ask." Next, I asked about galas and events he'd organized, funds he'd raised, donations and auction items he'd garnered, the number of volunteers, staff and vendors he'd managed. I also asked about his experience with planning annual budgets, writing grants, managing monthly financials, handling legal/liability and HR issues and answering to a board of directors.

By the end of our conversation, we identified some "gaps" in his experience, and he realized he didn't have all the qualifications for the job he wanted. That conversation also allowed us to put together a list of experiences he needed and an action plan of steps he could take to become more qualified. This changed the dialog from confrontation to cooperation because I was helping him achieve his goal...not standing in his way.

If they're astute, they'll also realize you've just demonstrated a coaching skill and a servant leader capacity that they want to learn and emulate. When I think back to my days of early leadership at Purina, I'm amazed that my leaders didn't fire me about three times a day, and I'm grateful for the sometimes pain-staking exercises they endured with me until "I discovered" the solution. Years later I also realized how much time, energy and just plain self-control that required. It's far easier and faster just to be directive and tell someone what to do, although it's also much less engaging and long lasting—which is critical to this generation. These coaching skills are the ones that build loyalty and develop leadership. As my leader would often remind me, "Good leadership is not efficient in the short term, but it's highly effective in the long term. We're in this for the long term."

This approach also works well with employees who believe they should receive the highest rating or merit increase year after year regardless of their actual performance or relative performance compared to their peers. I would begin by assuming their premise was correct and then ask, "As the top contributor, how have you exceeded all your goals? What have you done beyond your personal goals to help advance the enterprise or the business as a whole? Where have you contributed to the success of others?" These are good conversation starters and can help an employee quantify his or her achievements and focus beyond themselves to help others and the business succeed.

Whether you're developing future individual contributors or future leaders, the key is to help them define possible career paths and the skill sets they need to be prepared when the opportunity arises. Also keep in mind the value of having both individual contributors and leaders on your teams. One of my leaders used to remind us, "If you were all just alike, I'd only need one of you. I need ALL of you!" As we continue on to Chapter 2, we'll talk more about that diversity of thought and skill sets among team members and why it's so important to define and combine "strengths and shadows."

CHAPTER 2
GIVE ME STRAIGHT FEEDBACK

TRANSPARENCY, OR DOWNRIGHT HONESTY, DELIVERED in a productive and professional way, is one thing most employees look for in a leader. Millennials as a generation don't just look for it – they crave it. Getting an ongoing dose of straight feedback, both positive and constructive, is fundamental to their engagement and in turn, their commitment to the boss, to the job, and to the company. Think of straight feedback as a currency, or "bucks in the bank" if you will, that will pay dividends on relationships and performance.

In the best-case scenarios, we see employees given productive feedback become more trusting of leadership, more engaged in their jobs and more interested in doing good work, not just the minimum requirement. We also see employees sharing additional discretionary efforts, like speaking up more in meetings, offering ideas during discussions, volunteering to take on special projects or helping another team member with an assignment or skill development. At both Purina and Caterpillar, I witnessed that once employees felt "secure" that their leaders honestly knew them, genuinely cared for them, and wholeheartedly wanted to help them succeed, they blossomed– time and time again.

As leaders at Purina, part of our job was to develop a plan for engaging each employee. The plan included the actions we would take and even specifics about how and when we would take them to develop trust. Purina called these "trust milestones" – the milestones creating a foundation of trust. This is key because once you create a culture of trust, transparency is a natural extension. One builds on the other, as transparency continues to build trust while secrecy and rumors will erode trust.

So, for each employee, we outlined what success looked like as more and more mutual trust developed through "touchpoints" – saying or doing something that was personal to them. It may have been as simple as asking them about one of their family members or a recent vacation to treating them to their favorite coffee.

Then, we paid special attention to the results of those leadership outreaches. If a certain recognition or conversation really seemed to resonate with an employee, we made a note of it and repeated it. If not, we "course corrected" and tried another approach. (We'll talk more about this in Chapter 3 when we dive into employee recognition and the different "languages of appreciation.")

Here's an example of how to get started utilizing your touchpoints. When I worked at Purina, the leadership team had monthly "Touchpoint" meetings. We had a "round table" discussion where each leader took a turn talking about his or her team members individually, spotlighting their accomplishments, identifying skills they were developing and where they might need support, and then sharing something personal about the employee in terms of their families or hobbies or interests outside of work.

During the monthly "touchpoints meeting," each leader was assigned or volunteered to take responsibility for completing multiple touchpoints for various employees—some on their team and some on other leader's teams. Sometimes, they were supporting an employee with a skill development by inviting them to work on a project; or, they may have just agreed to congratulate an employee on a recent accomplishment and then report back to the team through a software similar to ones used to track customer contacts for sales or customer relationship management (CRM). We also made note of when employees were going on vacation or realizing a personal achievement (like running a half marathon) and multiple leaders (not just their immediate supervisor) made an effort to reach out to them personally with well wishes or congratulations. This amplified the knowledge of their accomplishments and further connected them with other leaders.

After my first meeting, I was exhausted just thinking about the number of touchpoints we'd made in the last month and the number we were planning for our employees for the next month. As we left the meeting, I told my boss, "I can't believe all the work that goes into this." He cocked his head to one side and said, "Did you think this all just happened? On its own?" "YES!" I answered with the wide-eyed look of a new supervisor. He smiled at my naivety (thank goodness) and went on to explain the importance of being intentional and sincere when it comes to knowing our people (a topic we'll learn more about in Chapter 3).

Of course, all this employee information is challenging to keep top of mind. Touchpoints can be managed in several ways. Although the CRM-type software worked well, I've also seen something as simple as leaders updating a spreadsheet that is shared by the leadership team. From an individual leader standpoint, I've seen leaders keep notes in their phones under each employee's name, and I've even seen the old-school notes on 3" x 5" cards that supervisors kept in their shirt pocket as they walked the production floor. They checked their notes before they walked down each aisle to remind themselves of people's names, what was important to them and sometimes what they had talked about before. Contrived? No. Intentional? Yes. Thoughtful? Absolutely. Regardless of how you collect and utilize this information, you can see that these are planned, repeatable behaviors with the express purpose of getting to know your employees and developing a culture of trust. In short, actions like these tell the team each person matters to you.

Now that we know the role trust plays in transparency, let's look at the specifics of giving straight feedback. We can break it down into three segments:

- Give me clear expectations & honest evaluations.
- Talk to me about my strengths and shadows.
- Be honest about my potential.

Let's look at each of these in more depth.

GIVE ME CLEAR EXPECTATIONS AND HONEST EVALUATIONS

Setting clear expectations is one of the most overlooked aspects of leadership and, in fairness, it's often overlooked because leaders believe they have done it. This is where an ongoing dialog with employees and checking for understanding are key. In short, employees want to know, "What do you want me to do?" and "How will you evaluate and compensate me?" A few basic steps that provide answers to these questions are:

- Review a job description (beyond the job posting) with specifics about the responsibilities
- Provide consistent training, standard work or processes for the basic tasks required
- Set three to five goals with a measurable outcome, timeline and definition of success
- Explain the compensation or reward structure.

While these are self-explanatory, the topic of "Where does my role fit in with the rest of the organization?" needs a little more discussion. Employees also want to know where they fit in the bigger picture of their department's success and the company's success. The millennial generation, in particular, wants to know that their company serves a larger purpose (We'll touch on that more in Chapter 6.) After they understand a company's purpose, they want to know how they can contribute and play a role in serving that larger purpose.

One of the most effective employee communication pieces I've seen to illustrate this concept was a **"Shared Goals"** document that was really just a piece of paper with three columns. A sample of this can be found in the **Leadership Tools Section** in the back of the book. The first column listed the company's purpose and top goals. The second column listed the department or work group's top goals in support of the company goals. The third column had blanks for the employee to fill in with his or her goals, and it had a section to explain how their work contributed to the success of the department and the company. This tool provided clear direction, and it challenged employees to identify how their individual work supported the larger purpose. Once they discovered the value of their work for themselves and could articulate it to their leader and other team members, they were more engaged and committed to their own success and the company's success.

Another leadership tool that is especially important to millennials is regular "One-on-One Discussions" (1:1) with their boss. Whether that's a daily 15-minute "huddle" or a weekly/bi-weekly 30-minute chat, that uninterrupted 1:1 time is critical. The commitment I made to my team members was they were the priority during this time – no phone calls, no emails, and "unless the place is burning down, no interruptions." This was time set aside to learn more about each other, celebrate wins and accomplishments, have honest conversations about anything that seemed overwhelming or confusing and organize action plans toward meeting goals. It was also an opportune time to complete the already identified leader touchpoints and discover new ones.

As I work with various companies, I find that many leaders don't do 1:1s because they don't have a structure to follow so it ends up being a "gripe" session or an awkward dialog. Either way, it's not something they want to repeat on a regular basis. Check with your Human Resources department to see if there is a standard format or protocol for leader/employee 1:1 meetings. If your company doesn't have a specified format, here's the "One-on-One Discussion" process that Purina used. We'll call it the "3-Bucket Exercise." Through the years, I have found it to be a universal tool, applicable across generations, cultures, languages and industries. I ask employees to come to the meeting with prepared responses to discussion topics organized in three "buckets:"

BUCKET 1: "AH-HA" (things I learned, completed, want to celebrate)

BUCKET 2: "Hmmmm" (things I'm aware of, want to learn more about, need an action plan for)

BUCKET 3: "What in the world?" (things I don't understand, didn't realize were part of the job or life in general or seem overwhelming)

In its simplest form, this format highlights what is going well and where employees need help. It also builds in time to celebrate successes, which we often move past too quickly, and it covers the short-term immediate needs as well as putting milestones in place to meet the longer-term quarterly or annual goals. Here's how it works.

Encouraging your team members to be brave enough to share the things that are overwhelming or speaking up if they don't even know where to start is the beginning of progress. That's Bucket 3. Once we identify those things then we can ask ourselves what it looks like when this problem is solved. Our answer defines our success. Then we ask ourselves what actions do we need to take to reach success? Those answers become the action plan we develop in Bucket 2. As we complete those action items in Bucket 2, we move them to accomplishments and something to celebrate in Bucket 1.

Why these three buckets? Tracking what employees learned or completed each week gives a sense of accomplishment, and it helps them realize they're making quantifiable progress. It also reinforces the thought, "If I mastered that, I can master this..." which may encourage them to take the next step toward a goal or take on a new project.

Identifying the issues they're aware of but haven't yet resolved is the first step to putting an action plan in place. I find that just helping them break down a large goal or hurdle into some smaller action steps propels them forward. Kelsey Meek, one of the Rock Star Millennials you'll meet in Chapter 4, said these meetings "organize the chaos in my mind and turn it into something constructive." I like that.

Some weeks there's little or nothing in Bucket 3 and some weeks it's loaded up! Either way, talking about the things that are overwhelming or frustrating is just plain healthy and honest. This is also the spot where employees would often talk about change—change in their job or at home and how best to deal with it. Employees also told me that giving overwhelming topics a place on our agenda legitimized them as real, reduced the stress of talking about them and opened dialog about how to fix them. It was also fun to watch things once deemed "overwhelming" move into Bucket 2 where we developed an action plan to overcome them and then move into a Bucket 1 list of accomplishments to be celebrated. The faster they saw this progression, the more apt they were to "'fess it and fix it."

In addition to covering the items in their "buckets," I also would have a list of follow up questions from previous discussions. At least once a month, we would touch on their progress toward personal and professional goals and how those moved them forward in their career planning.

Finally, we would end each discussion with the question, "What are you looking forward to?" which often became the first topic for our next meeting.

Sometimes leaders ask about discussing employee's personal life and whether that should be part of a 1:1 discussion with their leader. I follow the employees' lead here. Some want to talk about personal issues, particularly those related to managing work and home life, and others don't feel comfortable sharing at all. Either way is fine. I think there are times when solving a problem at home can help at work and vice versa. Here's an example:

Jackie McBrady was my first boss at Purina, and she was a young working mom, just like I was. During one of our weekly 1:1 discussions she asked what topics I had in Bucket 3 and I said, "Serving a healthy dinner to my family." She smiled a knowing smile as I explained that I liked to cook, and it was important for me to have a family dinner with our boys every evening, but it was hard to get it all organized. When I got home from work and hadn't seen the boys all day, I just wanted to spend time with them; yet, I wanted them to have a healthy meal. She gave me an assignment and asked me to answer the following questions:

- When do you have the most time and energy to cook?
- How much time do you want to spend preparing meals?
- Do you meal plan? If so, how?
- How many items/recipes do you prepare?
- What can you automate, delegate, or stop doing?

As I was completing my assignment, I learned a few things. I had the most time and energy to cook from 5-6am...not pm. In fact, I had no time or energy in the evening but that seemed like the logical time to prepare dinner, so the idea of meal prepping in the morning was a mindset shift. My son Ian was a baby at that time and awake by 5 a.m. so that early morning hour became my time alone with him. Win/win! Thirty minutes was the maximum amount of time I wanted to spend on meal prep and that included clean up. This decision affected my meal planning and shopping.

Instead of preparing three to five recipes for a meal, I chose one recipe and two sides—tops. I also decided those sides could be delegated, which meant I bought something already prepared or I opted for a fresh fruit or vegetable that required minimal effort. When I looked at what I could automate, I realized I was making multiple trips to the garbage can and could instead create a "garbage bowl" that I would empty once when I was finished. I also decided to stop stressing about a homemade meal every night and declare one night a week "a buffet" of leftovers or a "frozen meal" I could heat up.

Now, what does all of this have to do with leadership? First, I was excited to have this problem solved and my stress reduced. Immediately I was grateful to my leader for taking the time to help me, and I was sold on the process because I had already "proven" to myself it worked. To this day, I still do meal prep in the morning and pass along my lessons learned to other moms. Another thing Jackie taught me was how to use this line of questioning to break down a larger problem into an action plan that I could impact. In fact, as I took on more complicated projects at work, I found that I often repeated some of the same behaviors that I displayed in meal prepping.

To get me back on track, Jackie would ask, "Do you have too many recipes?" which was her way of asking if I was over-complicating the project....and usually the answer was, "Yes." She might also ask me if changing the timing on something would reduce the stress and improve the outcome...just like changing meal prep from evening to morning. Asking if there was something I could "automate, delegate or stop doing?" was another question that usually led to a breakthrough. (We'll talk about Timing & Thresholds more in Chapter 8 but this simple 1:1 discussion with my leader was the genesis of that tool for me.)

TALK TO ME ABOUT MY STRENGTHS AND SHADOWS

As leaders, it's much easier to talk to an employee about strengths than "areas of improvement, but honesty about improvement areas is important to millennials. So how can you frame the discussion in a way that makes you feel comfortable and gives employees the honest input they want? One approach I like is introducing the concept of strengths and shadows. I loved the positive posturing of shadows being skills that were in the background...or just weren't shining yet – as opposed to weaknesses that were to be avoided or hidden, or the sole focus of leadership improvement.

My shadows at the time were public speaking and strategic business knowledge or the ability to see a vision, articulate it in a way that brings others along and then design an executable plan to achieve the vision. That "shadows" discussion lead to a "how do we make them shine?" discussion, which was a positive approach to creating a Skills Development Plan, which we'll talk about in Chapter 4. For me, improving business acumen by attending higher-level leader meetings and developing better public speaking skills were two areas of focus. So, when I was given assignments in these areas, I understood it was for my development. This is also an example of direct, helpful feedback which leads to transparency and trust. We'll talk more about these types of assignments in Chapter 3.

Coaching Employees Through Shadow Development

To improve my business acumen or broader understanding of higher levels of leadership, my boss asked me to accompany him to some meetings with his peers. Once I attended a few meetings with him, he started giving me some very specific coaching. He worked with me on portraying confidence through the three S's: "**Space. Speech. Sight.**"

I hadn't considered some of the spatial nuances of meetings, but he gave me some practical tips regarding *Space* that I used the rest of my career –and shared with others. He coached me to always arrive early and take a seat at the table. If the seats were taken, he said to pull a chair into the room but pull it up to the table and make room for myself instead of sitting in the back of the room or along the conference room wall. He showed me how to take up additional space by placing my laptop or tablet on the table, along with my elbows. If there was an empty chair next to me once everyone was seated, he also coached me spread out even more by resting an arm on the back of the empty chair periodically to display confidence.

He also worked with me on my *Speech* patterns and tone. He explained that when we get emotional or passionate about something, we speak more quickly and at a higher pitch. He taught me to reverse this pattern by lowering my voice an octave... speaking more slowly... with intention...using fewer words. I found this counsel particularly effective in confrontational or crisis situations.

Sight for him was really about how I was viewed by others—what sight did they see? This went beyond professional dress and a "lean in" posture to include my facial expressions and the development of a poker face. He said, "You're very expressive and that serves you well as a leader. You're transparent and people trust you. That's a good thing, but you also need to learn how to have a poker face. As you advance in leadership, you need to be less transparent because whatever you're thinking shows right on your face. If you have a question, you squint your eyes and scrunch your forehead. If you agree with something you have a big smile. If you don't agree with something, you narrow your eyes and have a look of disapproval."

"So, I want you to go home tonight and practice in the mirror," he continued. "Practice making different faces in the mirror until you find one that is pleasant but doesn't express any clear emotion. When you get comfortable with what that looks like, I want you to practice doing it without the mirror so you know exactly what that expression feels like and can do it intuitively."

Following his direction, I practiced my neutral expression in the mirror that night and then did it without the mirror until I was comfortable with the transformation. For some reason, it helped me to put my hand in front of my face with my natural expression and then as I lowered my hand I would change to my neutral expression, the same way a mime goes from smiling to frowning. I practiced it so many times that I had forgotten I was using my hand at all.

The next morning, I walked proudly into his office to show him my expression transformation and you guessed it, I lowered my hand in front of my face as I changed my expression. I think he thought I was joking, so he asked me to do it a couple more times before he finally said, "The expression looks good. Lose the hand." As I look back now, this was comical and yet he continued to advise me on what I needed to say and do.

At some point during all this coaching, I got aggravated and told him that if I had to change my tone and speech and facial expression and the way I walk and sit and carry myself, maybe becoming a higher level leader just wasn't for me. I remember saying, "I feel like I'm trying to be someone I'm not."

He knew I had reached a threshold, so he suggested we take a break from coaching and take a walk in the park. As we walked, he asked me about my boys, who were one and four at the time and full of energy! He asked me what kinds of things they were doing and learning and then he asked, "Have they ever gotten hurt?" "Yes," I said, "not too long ago Shae got a splinter in his foot from the deck in the backyard, and I thought I might have to take him to the hospital because it was pretty big and deep. My husband was at work and the baby was asleep and I thought I'm just going to have to handle this myself."

He asked, "Were you scared?" And I said, "Yes, I was scared and sort of sick to my stomach because I didn't know if I could get the splinter out without hurting him or doing more damage." Then he asked, "Did you let Shae know you were scared?" I said, "No, I acted like it wasn't a big deal and suggested he take a bubble bath with extra bubbles, thinking if I could get him to soak in the tub I might be able to pull the splinter out with tweezers more easily and maybe without him really knowing it." "Did it work?" he asked. "Yep! Crisis averted."

He thought for a moment and then said, "So you were scared on the inside but calm on the outside so your son wouldn't be scared?" "Yes," I replied as I began to see where he was heading. "Kathryn that's all I'm asking you to do with these leaders," he said. "I'm not asking you to change who you are any more than you changed who you were with Shae. I'm simply asking you to choose to change your demeanor for an intended purpose...for a specific period of time." Lesson learned.

BE HONEST ABOUT MY POTENTIAL

In Chapter One, we talked about helping employees identify their career path as a leader or an individual contributor. Good leaders see the potential in employees that they may not see in themselves. Sometimes our job is to help them visualize themselves in a future role and let them see what you see as you paint a vivid picture for them. Conversely, if an employee seems to have an inflated opinion of themself or their skills, be honest about "the evidence" of those skills and what you've seen them demonstrate...or not demonstrate by denoting specific examples. It may be that they've demonstrated a skill periodically but not consistently. That's something else they can track, measure and improve. It's also ok to say you believe they have potential, but they will need to hone certain skills to reach that potential which leads to a development plan discussion.

One of the great leaders I worked for at Caterpillar was an example of someone who saw more potential in me than I saw in myself. I was a Communications & Learning Supervisor at the time, and I'd been in that position for four years, during which time I'd been the communicator for four different Vice Presidents. While we were having one of our career discussions, I told her I felt like I was working in my comfort zone, my boys were in grade school, and I just wanted to stay in that job for the rest of my career. She looked at me with a stern expression and said, "Not on my watch, you're not." Within a few months, she and another former leader of mine had a Global Marketing Manager position for me in our Logistics division, and they gave me a swift kick in the seat...and a move date. Period. End of story. I will always be grateful to both of them for seeing potential in me and pushing me beyond my comfort zone into another job that I ultimately loved and one that prepared me for my next few jobs at Caterpillar.

As leaders, sometimes it's important to give employees that nudge or help them see another way to advance. One of the women that I mentor works for a small business, and she wants to become a GM (general manager) at her company. In her world, all the GMs come up through the sales ranks, and she doesn't have a sales background. She went on to explain that "all" she had was an MBA with experience in finance, IT and HR which she didn't think qualified her to even apply for a GM role. The owner saw her as a future GM too, and we knew our challenge was to help her see herself as a GM and map out a different approach than sales to help her get there. Sometimes employees need to hear, "Yes you can do this. You're just going to do it differently."

We'll talk more about how to do this in Chapter 3 as we look at mentoring and coaching techniques and the role developmental assignments can play in advancing career paths.

CHAPTER 3
MENTOR AND COACH ME

MENTORING AND COACHING ARE OFTEN thought of as ancillary leadership skills—nice to have but not really practical unless your team is small and local, and you have lots of discretionary time as a leader. In fact, I found just the opposite to be true. The larger and more diverse my team, the more critical it was to coach them to grow individually and grow together as a team. I also found as I advanced in leadership and had less and less discretionary time, coaching my team became imperative for a couple of reasons.

First, developing team members builds a culture of trust. Your employees know when you're investing in them, making them a priority and setting them up to succeed. This generation, in particular, finds tremendous value in mentoring and more readily engages with leaders who make the investment.

Here's an example. When I had the privilege of being the project manager for the construction of the Caterpillar Visitors Center and assembling a team to run it once we opened, an employee approached me and asked to be on the team. She said, "I don't care what I do, I just want to work for you because I've watched people come out of your group and advance. I want to learn what you do and be one of those people." Humbling. We'll talk more about Servant Leadership and how it serves you in Chapter 8 but attracting top talent is a coveted outcome.

The second reason is that in addition to building a culture of trust, mentoring is contagious. When you help your employees become more successful and productive, they naturally want to help someone else too. This may manifest itself in support for you as their leader or in support for a team member or in going above and beyond for a customer. It's the "Pay It Forward" mentality—like paying for the coffee of the person behind you in line at Starbucks and watching the trickle-down effect as they do the same for someone else.

One of the books that was required reading for leaders at Purina was *The Customer Comes Second* by Hal Rosenbluth and Diane McFerrin Peters. The premise was that as leaders, if you have a culture focused on serving your people, they in turn will serve your customers and each other.[1] The result is a narrower focus and a broader return.

PUT YOUR PEOPLE FIRST
AND WATCH 'EM KICK BUTT.

– Hal Rosenbluth, author of The Customer Comes Second.

As these examples demonstrate, mentoring and coaching can take on many forms and be broad-based topics. What specifically are today's employees looking for when they say they want to be mentored? Three specific things:

- Help me see the potential you see.
- Provide sincere recognition and redirection.
- Give me developmental work and tell me why.

Now, let's look at each of these individually and identify some specific actions you can take.

HELP ME SEE THE POTENTIAL YOU SEE

When I went to work at Purina, I began to understand the depth and breadth of seeing potential in people. In fact, this company was created on that very premise, as I learned at orientation.

My first day at Purina was like none I had experienced before or have experienced since. I'm sure we completed all the required paperwork but what I remember most was the way I felt when I was there. I felt like I was home. They began orientation by sharing the story about the origin of Purina, a company that was founded by William H. Danforth. He was an independently wealthy man and in the 1950s, he created the Youth Foundation in St. Louis for "wayward youth." He found that once he got these kids out of gangs, or out of prison, or off drugs, no one would hire them. So, he created a company to hire these kids: Purina.

He also wrote a book during that time, called *I DARE YOU*. The premise is, "I Dare You to be the best you can be and then help someone else do the same." We all received a copy of the book in which Danforth explains what makes Purina different: "We cherish our people." Not like them. Not tolerate them, but we CHERISH our people. [2]

When you think of the word "cherish," what do you think of? I think of something priceless...rare...a keepsake. Something to hold dear. That's how they felt about their employees...and I felt it, even on the first day. Cherished.

They went on to say the company's purpose was "Developing people for life." And added, "Never confuse what we make with why we're here. Because what we make will change, but our purpose will not. We're here to develop people for life." At the time, Purina made Hostess Twinkies® and Ding Dongs®, Eveready Batteries®, and Beech-Nut® Baby Food, along with cereals and pet food. True to their logic, many of those things they no longer produce today – and, they have added many new products since that day.

Another insight they shared at orientation was, "We hire bright, smart people and we don't expect them to be here long. Our job is to send them off better than we found them, and with a positive impression of Purina. Why? When they leave here, they may work for another Fortune 50 company. They may be in a position to impact a merger or acquisition. They can buy and sell our stock, and at the very least, when they go to the grocery store, they can buy dog food, and we want it to be Purina." My response? WOW! I remember thinking, "I am never leaving this company. I'm home."

Let's think about the genesis of Purina and how it applies to today's workforce. What message was Danforth sending when he created a company with the singular intent to hire "wayward youth?" Talk about seeing potential! He didn't see those kids for what they *were* – when no one would hire them. Instead, he saw them for who they *could be* and then helped them get there. Both pieces of this equation are critical.

Today's employees are looking for the same thing. They want leaders who see the best in them, who see the potential they may not see, and then help them not only see that potential for themselves but attain it too. Neal Lewis was one of the great bosses I had at Purina, and he used to say, "At best, mentors are mirrors. We don't create anything that isn't already there. We just help you see what we see."

This culture of "seeing potential" and "developing people for life" was captured and cultivated through Purina's 360-degree mentoring program. Part of new employee onboarding was meeting a "leader mentor" and a "peer mentor" who would help you in your early days on the job. New employees were told that within 90 days they would be mentoring because at Purina, "everybody mentors." Everyone was a mentor and a mentee.

Although my peer mentor supported me as a "buddy" while I was getting acclimated at Purina, my leader mentor was Lynn Reinacher, and she stayed with me my entire career—not my career at Purina but my ENTIRE CAREER. Yes, she helped me solve business problems at Caterpillar. Not once or twice. She helped me for 22 YEARS, until I retired and then she was one of my biggest cheerleaders as I started my own mentoring business. Lynn is the epitome of a mentor and was the embodiment of "developing people for life." She offered the perfect combination of encouragement, honest feedback and sound advice.

I remember calling Lynn one day, not long after I started working at Caterpillar. I was trying to initiate a mentoring program like the one I had experienced at Purina, and I was way out of my element as an entry level marketing person trying to initiate an HR program. I was frustrated that I wasn't getting traction and called Lynn to complain. When I told her I was mentoring others but couldn't get a program started, her response was, "Is that why you DID IT? Did you mentor people for the sole purpose of starting a program?"

"Of course not," I responded. Then she asked, "Why did you DO IT? Why did you mentor those people?" I answered, "Because there was a need and I knew how. Just like I learned at Purina. If you have the Ability, you have the Responsibility." She responded, "DONE. If your driver was to be recognized, then you need a program. If your driver was to truly help others, then you've done that. DONE." Our conversation was the genesis of the "**Did it. Do it. Done.**" tool you'll find in the Tool Section in the back of the book, and I used it many times throughout my career. Another time I remember calling Lynn when I was having a tough day and I said, "I want you and Neal to make a place for me. I want to come back to Purina." Lynn answered, "We didn't train you up to come back. We trained you up to go forward. Are there change agents to mentor? Teams to build? Leaders to support?" I answered "Yes" to all three questions, and she said, "Then you have good work to do there. GO – I Dare You." As we hung up, I laughed and cried and never again looked back because Lynn had taught me my focus was forward.

If mentoring is something you'd like to start at your company, you can begin by working with your local HR folks to identify employees who want to be mentors and those who want to be mentored. Matching mentors and mentees can be done more formally through assignments or it can be the result of informal networking once interested mentors and mentees have identified themselves. I've even seen pairings done through a "speed dating"-type exercise which is fun, too.

What if your company doesn't have a formal mentoring program or matching system but you would like to be a mentor and help others—where do you start? I began by reaching out to new hires. Because there were so few women at Caterpillar at the time, whenever I saw a new employee announcement for a female, I reached out to her and asked if she had a mentor or would like one. If she was interested, we would arrange an introductory meeting or coffee chat and go from there. These women often asked how they could repay the kindness and each time I asked them to help someone else, which they usually did. I also found the reason many women didn't mentor was because they didn't have a process to follow or tools to share and our meetings gave them both.

Once mentors and mentees have been paired, the structure for mentoring conversations can follow the same Bucket 1,2,3 format we reviewed for 1:1 discussions in Chapter 2. When you enter into a mentoring relationship, it's also good to establish some guidelines to determine: how frequently you will meet (weekly or bi-weekly is preferred); how many sessions you will schedule (minimum of 4, maximum of 12); where you will meet, and how much time you will dedicate to each session (typically 30-60 minutes). Sometimes meeting in a more casual setting like a coffee shop is preferred and with more and more employees working remotely, a virtual coffee chat may be another alternative. We'll talk more about working remotely in Chapter 5. You'll also find a list of **"Mentor/Mentee Discussion Topics"** in the Tool Section in the back of the book to get you started.

PROVIDE SINCERE RECOGNITION AND REDIRECTION

Part of the mentoring and coaching that today's employees are looking for includes sincere recognition and redirection. This often turns into a guessing game for leaders until we better understand our individual team members and what makes them tick. I've found the most effective and efficient approach is to just ask them –and the sooner the better.

In fact, during my first meeting with a new employee or a new mentee, I review the same four topics from the Discussion Topics Tool (found in the Leadership Tools section in the back of the book), including: 1)"Getting to Know You,"2) "Recognition," 3)"Vision & Values," and 4)"Success." Why? Two reasons. First, when an employee or mentee is new to the role, they're full of energy and enthusiasm and focused on building a positive relationship with you so it's the perfect time to learn more about them and understand how you can best support them going forward. Second, the sooner you understand how to tailor recognition and redirection specifically for them, the farther and faster they will advance.

Let's look at each one of these in a little more detail to understand the value of the information you're gathering and how to apply it.

...

1. **GETTING TO KNOW YOU:** Tell me about you personally—your family, your personal favorites (food, activities, books, music, shows, travel)? What do you like to do outside of work? Describe your best boss, best day at work and worst day at work. What would have made your worst day better?

Why is this important? On the most basic level, you're communicating that you care enough about this individual to get to know them, beyond what's on their resume. You may also find common interests where you can connect. (Think back to touchpoints from Chapter 1.) The important thing here is to touch on a shared connection or acknowledge that you like the same activity and then turn the conversation back to them. As my leader used to remind me, "It's all about them." "What is?" I had asked. "Everything," he said. He had witnessed me "taking over the conversation" during an earlier new hire discussion and afterward he said to me, "You'd better be warming up to sing because all I heard during that discussion was ME ME ME." Lesson learned.

Asking employees to describe their best boss gives you insight into how they like to be led and what's important to them. If an employee says, "My best boss gave me a goal and then left me alone to do it," the employee doesn't want to be micromanaged; that opens the door for a later discussion about how to best update one another to create a balance between your need for information and the employee's need for autonomy.

If someone's best day at work is one where they got everything done on their "To Do" list, that person may be more task oriented than someone whose best day involved multiple meetings with interesting people. (We'll revisit some of this information again in Chapter 8 when we learn about the "Timing & Thresholds" tool.) Asking about a bad day at work further defines their preferences, but the greatest insight comes with the answer to the next question, "What would have made that bad day better?"

I learned this lesson when I was a Communications & Learning Manager at one of the Caterpillar tractor factories. We wanted to change the culture in certain areas of the shop floor, and I interviewed some of our production folks on all three shifts to better understand their needs.

I asked these same "getting to know you" questions, and they often quantified a "bad day" as one where their line was down or they didn't get the materials they needed to meet their production goal. I half-heartedly asked, "What would have made that bad day better?" knowing the answer was "Getting the parts out and making my production goal"—right? Wrong. I was so wrong.

The answer consistently – line by line, shift by shift, worker by worker – was, "It would have been better if my boss would have come by to say, 'Hey, I know you're doing your best. Keep at it.'" I was floored and grateful for their honesty. This ultimately changed the direction of future communications and the development of our leader training.

...

2. **RECOGNITION:** How do you like to be recognized? When someone demonstrates "genuine concern" for you, what does it look like? One good resource here is Gary Chapman's *5 Languages of Appreciation in the Workplace*. (They include: Words of Affirmation, Quality Time, Acts of Service, Tangible Gifts and Physical Touch.)[3] Of these five, what behavior is the most authentic for you?

Why is this important? Even the most well-intentioned leaders can experience "recognition backfire" when recognition is delivered in the wrong way or at the wrong time for an employee. This is one area where the "Golden Rule" does not apply. Instead of recognizing someone the way YOU would like to be recognized, follow the "Platinum Rule" and recognize them the way THEY would like to be recognized. Ask them. They know, and they'll tell you. After you know what "language" and behavior speaks to them and act on it, you'll notice the "touchpoints" being more effective with less effort because they are so targeted to that employee.

...

3. **VISION AND VALUES:** What is your vision for this job? What do you want to get out of this experience? What excites you about it? How does this job fit with your career vision? What are your personal values? What are you passionate about?

Why is this important? Understanding their values and what they are passionate about is GOLD. Pure GOLD. Whether they value creativity, authenticity, fun, service, knowledge or kindness, their values are demonstrated in the work they do and the way they interact with others. Recognizing that value as a strength in them and commenting when you see it demonstrated is affirming and engaging. For example, I had a leader who would bring me into a meeting and preface it by saying, "I need to borrow your creativity for about 20 minutes." I was immediately affirmed and energized, and my brain would tend to click into a creative overdrive with something as simple as his acknowledgment.

...

4. SUCCESS: Why do you want to succeed? Why do you want this company/organization to succeed?

Why is this important? The answer here may range from something as fundamental as "I need to pay my bills" to something more altruistic like "Our company builds a better world, and I want to be part of that." Either way, an employee's response can help you as a leader frame goals to align with their purpose which at some point may be just the impetus they need to move forward. Here's an example.

My first supervisory role at Purina was leading a creative group of writers, designers and layout folks who prepared projects for on-line and print production. At the time I began leading the group, these were three distinct sections, each with its own manual operations. My charge was to unite these groups through a single on-line platform which would make the whole department more efficient and productive.

I knew each day that I delayed in achieving this transformation I was costing the department and the company money, but I didn't know where to begin. To me this was a technology puzzle, and I was just plain stuck. During each 1:1 discussion, my boss would ask about my progress, and I would recite the latest research I'd done about the various platforms. I was in a "paralysis by analysis" mode. One day instead of reviewing my research, he suggested we take a walk outside for our 1:1 discussion. He also knew that a walk outside was one of three things that revitalized me. (We'll talk more about this in Chapter 7.)

During our walk, we re-visited my purpose. He recalled that I wanted to succeed in this job to build a better department for the next generation. He also recalled that I wanted Purina to succeed because I wanted my son to work there. Then he took it one step further and asked, "What if by chance when Shae grows up, he comes to work here and just happens to lead this department. Is it ready for Shae? Is the equipment there? The technology? The training? What would you need to do to set Shae up to succeed?"

In an instant, my mind was reeling with ideas, and I knew exactly what to do. I told him we needed to convert all the workstations from PCs to Macs and train all the staff on design software so they could go directly to on-line display or print. He asked what resources I needed? How long it would take and what it would cost? I had the answers to all his questions from my research, and within minutes I'd gone from a standstill to a full out sprint. I even remember telling him I didn't have time to walk any longer because I had so much work to do. He waved me on and said we'd catch up the next time. Amazing leader!

Within weeks, the transformation had happened. Our turnaround time per project had improved, our project costs had decreased, our customer satisfaction scores had increased, and the team morale had improved with the investment in equipment and training. We all felt like we'd stepped up our game, and I was so proud of our team for the way they had championed this change. Even though I was credited for meeting the goal, I knew my leader was the one to thank for spurring me to action by simply framing the discussion according to my purpose. Brilliant.

Making Redirection Positive

We've talked a lot about recognition and the role it plays in engaging and empowering employees. Now, let's spend a little time on redirection, and you'll see that a lot of the same concepts apply. If you remember our discussion on "straight feedback" in Chapter 2, today's employees want transparency. I've found that some of the same framing that works well with recognition also works well with redirection. Following are a couple examples of talking points or framing statements I've learned from skilled leaders and have used repeatedly:

"WE BOTH WANT THE SAME THING AND THAT'S FOR YOU TO SUCCEED. NOW, LET'S FIGURE OUT THE NEXT STEPS TO GET YOU THERE."

Framing feedback in a way that aligns with an employee's values or sense of purpose is a good place to start. Once you're on common ground, "we both want you to succeed," helping them focus on moving forward is the next step.

"WHEN I LOOK AT THE SKILLS YOU'VE DEMONSTRATED, I'VE SEEN _____, _____ AND _____. THE SKILLS GAP I SEE IS _____. LET'S GET FOCUSED ON CLOSING THAT GAP BECAUSE _____ IS A SKILL YOU'LL NEED TO ADVANCE."

This dialog is transparent. It affirms the demonstrated skills and identifies a skill that is lacking, separating the skill from the person. It also frames the reason for improving the skill, which is advancement. The underlying message here is you have faith in this employee. You see a future for him or her, and you want to help them develop this skill to advance. From this point, it's easier to brainstorm with the employee about possible next steps or an action plan to acquire the required skill.

"THE LEADERSHIP I'M LOOKING FOR
FROM YOU IS_____."

This one tells the employee that you see them as a leader and you're asking them to improve a specific skill. As a punctuation point, one leader added, "This is going to hold you back," which got my attention. At the time, I had a temper and a sharp tongue, and he let me know there was no place for either one in leadership.

"WE'VE REACHED A POINT WHERE WE NEED TO
CHANGE THE PEOPLE OR CHANGE THE PEOPLE."

This is particularly appropriate when you have an employee or a group resistant to change. The statement lets them know you are at a crossroad as a leader; change of one kind or another is imminent. It's also clear they have a choice to make.

Finally, if you have an employee who has the skill set to do the work but is not taking the initiative or is waiting for "permission," here's a leadership statement to use:

"IF YOU SEE SOMETHING THAT NEEDS TO BE DONE AND
YOU HAVE THE ABILITY TO DO IT, YOU ALSO HAVE THE
RESPONSIBILITY. IT'S THAT SIMPLE."

I learned this lesson at Purina during a time when the company had launched a "My Purina" learning program for employees. As part of the training, employees learned about the manufacturing and distribution of products as well as consumer buying habits. We learned what differentiated our products and had talking points to share with friends and family or even fellow shoppers at the grocery store. We also had pet food coupons to share which made us very popular! As employees, we became Purina advocates to the general public, and I remember feeling empowered to share our message. The feeling of empowerment was captured in the "My Purina" slogan but it also permeated inside and outside the office. Here's how my leader put a finer point on it.

One day when my boss and I were solving problems while taking one of our walks, he reached down and picked up a piece of trash and kept walking. I remember saying to him, "You're a director of this company. You shouldn't be picking up trash." He said in response, "Kathryn, if you don't understand why I picked up that trash, you really don't understand the concept of 'My Purina.' This is my company, and it's your company. If you see something that needs to be done and you have the <u>ability</u> to do it, you also have the <u>responsibility</u>. It's that simple."

GIVE ME DEVELOPMENTAL WORK AND TELL ME WHY

Three of the most impactful words you can say to today's employees are, "and here's why." They're interested in what you're thinking but equally, if not more, interested in why you're thinking it. Remember this generation has grown up with collaborative leadership and is accustomed to participating in decision making.

Part of that collaborative leadership can be employees "leading upward" or providing feedback about your leadership style. First, you have to ask yourself honestly if you're open to that type of dialog. If you're not, there's no need to introduce it. If you are, it can be priceless—much more effective than anonymous comments on an annual employee opinion survey, and here's why.

During these transparent discussions, employees often share what appeals to them about your leadership style and what they find intriguing about a leadership tool or approach they've learned through a podcast, social media post, audio book or a peer who works at another company. Although the ultimate decision whether or not to incorporate the feedback is yours, their ability to share it is empowering and gives you insight into how they would like to be led or what inspires them.

By the same token, when you tell them what you want them to do and why it's important for them or the business or both, that's also empowering to them and gives them insight into your leadership logic, which expedites the process

So far in this chapter, we've talked about sharing the potential you see in employees and sharing honest recognition and redirection. Whether you're working with an employee to further hone an existing skill or develop a new one, outlining specific assignments and relating the assignment to the employee's skill development is key. Here's an example:

About three years after I started working at Purina, my husband was transferred and had an opportunity to become a partner in a small business – his ultimate dream as an entrepreneur. Neal Lewis was my boss at that time, and he had been such an amazing leader to me that I dreaded telling him I was leaving. I told him about my husband's opportunity and his first reaction was to be thrilled for Scott's success. Think about that: his first reaction. He knew me, he knew my husband, he knew that was Scott's dream, and he was thrilled for Scott. He was a true servant leader, one who led by example.

His second reaction was to call in his administrative assistant and ask her to set up a whole litany of meetings for me with other leaders in multiple departments, including accounting, legal, HR, and Mergers & Acquisitions. He also asked her to include me in some meetings with Neal and his peers. I was dumbfounded and thought I must not have been clear in my communication. Then I said, "Neal, I must not have been clear; we're being transferred. I'm leaving Purina."

He answered, "I know. How long do you think it will take you to sell your house?" I answered 3-6 months. He said, "That's perfect! I want you to tell your mentor, but no one else. We'll tell your team and our customers when the time for you to leave gets closer. Right now, you and I have a lot of work to do. I'm setting up several meetings to give you some of the experiences you'll need. I want you to meet with our accounting folks and better understand higher level budgets and get more practice with department level P&Ls. You'll be meeting with HR and Legal to understand some of the cases we're involved in and why. You're going to meet with the Mergers & Acquisitions group and join me in some meetings with my peers to get a feel for the discussions and interactions at the Director level. Make sense?"

I said, "No, it doesn't make sense. I'm not a Director. I'm a Marketing Communications Manager. I thought I'd spend my whole career here but now I'm not. Why are you doing this?" He answered, "You're right. You're not a Director now, but you will be some day. You just won't do it here. And when you get to that level at some other Fortune 50 company, you will need to know these things, and it's my job to prepare you. I thought I had the rest of my career to teach you, but we only have a few months so let's get busy."

What happened here? A culmination of everything we've talked about in this chapter. Neal saw the potential in me, helped me to see it, identified the gaps where I needed growth and gave me assignments to gain some of those experiences for my development. Throughout this learning journey, I was reminded again that "developing people for life" wasn't a slogan at Purina, it was a commitment, an investment, and a legacy – one that I was grateful for and happy to pass along to others.

As we move into Chapter 4, we'll dive deeper into the practice of developing employees and the role sponsorship can play in succession planning and career development.

CHAPTER 4

SPONSOR ME FOR FORMAL DEVELOPMENT

ON THE SURFACE, **SPONSORSHIP SEEMS** like an easy task for us as leaders. Those of you who have done this and done it well, know it can be time consuming and sometimes frustrating. Let's look at some different ways to approach this to deliver the most success for your employees, their sponsors and you.

If you work in a smaller company, you may be an employee's boss and sponsor. Sam Heer is the owner of two Renewal by Andersen® locations in Illinois and Iowa, and he is a great example of a small business owner who is both a boss and a sponsor for his young leaders. He has invested in on-going mentoring for his female managers, supervisors and customer-facing staff. He has worked with other owners to provide benchmarking opportunities for his team and included his leaders in corporate pilot programs and leadership development offerings. Through his sponsorship, his leaders have expanded their network and broadened their understanding of the business and the industry.

During my initial discussions with Sam about mentoring, I asked, "What business problems are we trying to solve?" In that discussion, Sam said he wanted to continue to grow the business and expand the number of locations.

He identified two women leaders as being pivotal to that growth and pinpointed specific projects that he wanted them to lead. When asked, "What's preventing them from doing this?" he responded, "confidence." He knew they had the potential and skillsets they needed, and my job was to instill confidence, help them map out an action plan, and be their accountability partner to help them meet those goals in a matter of months. The women who

Sam Heer (left), Amber Kienast (center) and Kelsey Meek (right) attended the Renewal by Andersen Leadership Summit. Note: you'll learn more about Amber in Chapter 5.

did just that are shining examples of Rock Star Millennials and what they can accomplish! Let's meet one of those Rock Star Millennials, Kelsey Meek, and see what we can learn from her.

KELSEY MEEK

AS THE BUSINESS Manager at Renewal by Andersen, Central Illinois and Quad Cities, Kelsey Meek leads the Finance, Human Resources and Information Technology departments. Sam saw Kelsey as a future General Manager (GM) for his business and encouraged her to create her own path to becoming a GM, since this position typically advances through sales. As part of her development, he challenged her to take on projects that spanned multiple departments and benefited the com-

Kelsey Meek is the Business Manager at Renewal by Andersen of Central Illinois and Quad Cities, and the proud mother of Ava.

pany as a whole. His purpose here was to give her a more well-rounded perspective and a working knowledge of many departments beyond the financials.

One of her goals was to update the company's IT platform with a solution that offered additional security, backup capabilities and improved integration with the existing finance, production and sales data. Not only did Kelsey meet this goal in record time, she did it on the heels of finishing her MBA and giving birth to her first child!

Another multi-departmental goal Kelsey accomplished was redesigning the office space and relocating all back office and sales personnel, in addition to re-purposing the warehouse space to create an in-house paint and stain shop. She worked closely with the Production Manager to expand this in-house capability that reduced outsourcing costs, increased quality and improved turn-around times.

She also spent some time working in the paint shop to better understand the processes and get to know the production folks. During her time there, she learned from the team how to best reduce "paperwork" and ultimately moved to digital processing done on iPads. Her "hands on" work earned the respect of the production team, and the automated paperwork stream-lined job processing for the Production Manager. An added benefit for her finance team was the automated process also moved jobs through the system faster and on to billing, which improved revenue realization times.

From an HR perspective, the new paint and stain shop required the creation of additional in-house training and safety protocols, including on-going safety meetings, which Kelsey organized and conducted in collaboration with the Production Manager.

In addition to giving her projects such as these, Sam included Kelsey in strategic planning meetings with all of his department heads to give her a better overall picture of how the departments fit together. Being involved in these meetings was a turning point for Kelsey – one that helped her see the people and processes behind the financials in their respective departments. Clearly, her exposure to these projects and experience in managing them gave her an expanded view of her Finance Manager role and her potential for advancement.

What was Kelsey's thought about being groomed for a future GM? "I'm grateful that Sam saw that potential in me and continues to give me opportunities to grow. For me, mentoring was part of that growth. I would barely allow myself to think about becoming a GM let alone say it out loud, but having a mentor helped me voice my dream and then put a plan to it."

Kelsey is a Rock Star Millennial with a well-developed combination of talent. She is a servant leader who sees the long-term vision for the company, easily articulates that vision to bring others along and then empowers teams to execute a plan to get there. Amazing.

Mentors and Sponsors

The terms mentors and sponsors are sometimes used interchangeably, but in my experience their purposes are distinct. Mentors are enlisted to coach and develop employees at various points and positions throughout their career, while considering externalities of home life, social life, etc. A sponsor's intended purpose is to advance the employee's career. Period. This is done by being an employee's advocate and recommending them for current open positions or special projects or placing in the queue for succession planning.

Because sponsors are putting their reputation on the line as they promote an employee, they often prefer to have a "working experience" with that employee. This experience may come from having the employee directly report to them so they see the employee's work firsthand or it may come from involvement in a project or a "special assignment." We'll talk more about the logistics of this later in this chapter. Sponsors can be part of a formal program or they can be informal. Let's take a look at each one and how they might operate.

Formal Sponsorship Programs

In larger companies, bosses, mentors and sponsors may be three very different people who work together to advance an employee's career. Given this scenario, the employee's boss is typically the one who spearheads the plan and enlists the help of other leaders. As a boss, you may be in a position to sponsor an employee for a promotion or align someone for succession planning within your group, but helping them advance beyond your prevue often requires the support of others.

Before you begin the process of seeking out a sponsor for your employee, check with your Human Resources (HR) department to see if there is a formal sponsorship process in place. This can be as simple as a matching system among high-level leaders and high-performing employees with similar career paths (accounting, marketing, manufacturing), much like some companies match mentors and mentees.

If a formal process is available and has an existing structure that has been successful, work within the structure. If you know leaders who are sponsors and/or have been sponsored through this system, talk to them to better understand how the system works and why it was successful for them. HR may have a list of folks who would be willing to share their personal experiences too. This anecdotal information is good to pass along to your employees who are looking for a sponsor and want to learn from others who have participated in the program.

If there are requirements the employees must meet or agree to before they can be considered for sponsorship, those requirements should also be shared with employees so they are aware of the considerations, which may or may not fit with their life or career plan at a certain point in time.

For example, when I was working at Caterpillar as the Communication Manager in the tractor factory, I was recruited for a Global Marketing Manager position in our external Logistics segment. At the time, the position served our global customer base and required 80% travel, primarily to Europe and Asia. I had two young boys in grade school and didn't want to travel that much or that far consistently, so I declined being considered for the position and explained why.

Two years later, I was recruited for the same position, but some things had changed. First, the position had evolved. There were teams in Europe, Asia and North America, and this position managed those teams. Second, the Global travel was still required but it was much less than 80%. Third, my boys were two years older and more self-sufficient which made it easier for me to travel. Finally, I had a different boss who was focused on broadening my career, and as I mentioned in Chapter 2, she "highly encouraged" me to take the role when she gave me a move date and posted my job. God bless her.

Requirements for sponsorship may include accessibility like being globally mobile to travel, as in my example, or they may include being willing to relocate domestically or internationally. They might also be performance based and require that candidates have achieved the highest level of employee performance evaluations based on exceeding goals for multiple years. Sponsors may also value diverse experience and may be looking for candidates who have had multiple varied assignments in the field or in a functional capacity or both.

An employee may be willing or able to meet some of these requirements but not others, especially if they are part of a dual-income household. For example, an employee may be able to travel internationally but only able to re-locate domestically.

This was a conversation I had multiple times with various leaders throughout my career at Caterpillar. Not only were we a dual-income family, my husband owned a small business and had partners. So, relocating for us wasn't a matter of my husband giving a two-week notice at his job or working remotely. He would have had to dissolve a partnership and sell out of a business. I understood my limited mobility impacted my opportunities at some points, so I was even more focused on being able to travel and lead global teams and volunteer for special projects that would provide diverse experiences.

If your company doesn't have a formal sponsorship program or a good access point for leaders to connect on the topic, how else can you support an employee's career development? Helping an employee seek out informal sponsorship by connecting them with other resources is another avenue. The next section touches on some examples of outreach, many of which your employee can drive with the help of your direction.

Informal Sponsorship

If you're a leader in a small business, one resource for employee sponsorship may be through Small Business Development Centers (SBDC) in your area. There are more than 1000 of these nationwide, and they are federally funded by the Small Business Administration (SBA), with additional sponsorship often provided through local universities. The SBA also funds SCORE, which is a group of current and retired business leaders and entrepreneurs who volunteer their time to mentor or sponsor. A good exercise for an employee in search of a sponsor may be to ask them to research local universities, business development centers and groups like SCORE to identify potential sponsors and then work with you as their leader to develop an outreach plan.

If your business is a member of an organization like the Chamber of Commerce or the National Association of Women Business Owners (NAWBO), there may be informal opportunities for your employees to connect with would-be sponsors. NAWBO also offers "MasterMind" groups where a small subset of members meet on a regular basis in a confidential forum to discuss business issues and help each other problem solve. MasterMind groups are becoming more and more popular in a variety of industries and are another avenue for connecting employees with seasoned professionals who could provide informational interviews, job shadowing, or informal sponsorship opportunities.

Sometimes the best alternative for an employee is encouraging them to use a combination of both formal and informal sponsorships. Although coordinating all the pieces may be more time consuming, the result can be customized for each employee's needs. Lauren Carroll is another Rock Star Millennial and a good example of someone who sought out a combination of informal and formal sponsorship to support her career advancement. Let's see what we can learn from her.

LAUREN CARROLL

Lauren Carroll,
Executive Director
at the Sexual Assault
Resource Center
(SARC) in Bryan/
College Station, TX

LAUREN CARROLL IS a Rock Star Millennial and the Executive Director of the Sexual Assault Resource Center (SARC) in Bryan/College Station, TX. Although her degree was in Political Science, she was recruited for an internship in social work which changed the course of her career. After witnessing the work of folks who served as a guardian ad litem for her clients, she soon realized she could have a greater impact on the outcome of people's lives as an attorney, so she went to law school.

After law school, she interned with an organization where she was guardian ad litem for abused children and went on to be a trial lawyer representing abused women in domestic violence cases. In hindsight, Lauren's two internships not only provided unique experiences that changed her career path, but they also introduced her to women who would become her mentors and sponsors going forward. In her current role, Lauren reports to a board of directors instead of a single boss, so she needed to look beyond her immediate circumstances for sponsorship. Lauren sought out three mentors and asked them to take on the role of sponsors to help advance her career.

Lauren's first sponsor was Elizabeth Cotellese, a social worker and the Director of Baby University in Chattanooga, TN. This program supports young mothers in parenting skills and provides everyday needs to families. Lauren met Elizabeth at a networking event and was subsequently recruited for an internship with the Southeast Tennessee Development District to lead a program called, "Relatives Raising Kids in Foster Care." Elizabeth trained Lauren for the role and then began grooming her to be the director of an agency someday. "Her passion made me want to do the internship and then take on more," Lauren said. "She wanted me to be bigger than she was, and she encouraged me to go to law school because she knew that would lead to bigger things for me." Elizabeth saw potential in Lauren and has been a consistent mentor and sponsor as Lauren grew to become the Executive Director that Elizabeth envisioned years ago.

Lauren's second sponsor is Magistrate Kimber Strawbridge in Jacksonville, FL who had been a lawyer for the Guardian ad Litem Program. Lauren recalled, "She was my supervisor, and I tried my first case under her. She was instrumental in moving me forward when the Executive Director position came open in Texas. She wanted me to go beyond being a trial lawyer and helped me see a larger career path for myself."

As her third mentor and sponsor, I structured my role with Lauren to focus on teambuilding skills, management processes and insights for her board of directors. She quickly became skilled in advocacy and media relations, as she worked closely with state and local government officials and news outlets. Early in this assignment Lauren recalled, "As a trial attorney, my success was very clear cut, and the feedback was immediate. I either won or lost the case. In the non-profit world, success isn't as defined or as immediate."

Lauren's success in her current role is measured by services provided, grants secured, and donations raised in addition to developing partnerships with state and local agencies and securing sponsorship from community leaders. "Leading a non-profit is very different than working in a corporation," Lauren said. "Many of my employees have been through a trauma so leading them requires humanitarian practices and management skills. Our clients are in crisis, so you have to assess each situation quickly and apply critical thinking immediately because someone's life is at stake."

Having seen the lasting value of mentors and sponsors in her own career, Lauren created an internship program at SARC and seeks out candidates who would provide value to the agency but would also benefit from her sponsorship in years to come. How does she view this opportunity? "As I look at these young women and men, I know this is one way I can impact their future and change their trajectory, just like my mentors did for me."

Whether you are leading or mentoring or sponsoring young employees, take time to have the conversation with them so you can understand their personal situation and you don't inadvertently volunteer them for something that isn't feasible and backfires for both of you. Also make them aware of any requirements for sponsorship so they can make a fully informed decision. If you're their boss, take time to make other leaders or potential sponsors aware of an employee's limitations as well as their skillsets and experience at the onset of the discussions. These honest discussions on both fronts are evidence of your transparency, which builds trust with employees and potential sponsors.

Skills Development Plans v. Performance Improvement Plan

If an employee would like to be sponsored but is missing key experiences or knowledge, think back to our discussion in Chapter 3 about evaluating "gaps" and help them create a **Skills Development Plan*** so the employee is qualified to be considered a viable candidate if the opportunity for sponsorship arises. This plan may also include a Developmental Assignment, where the employee takes a lateral move or even a downgrade for a short period of time to acquire a critical skill or experience.

I saw this multiple times when I worked in the tractor factory area at Caterpillar. Employees might take a second- or third-shift supervisory role to get the "shop floor leadership" experience. Or someone from engineering might work in assembly to better understand how the 'designed parts' came together on the assembly line.

These types of 'hands on" assignments expanded an employee's knowledge and skill set and improved collaboration and the flow of ideas between the sponsoring group and the receiving group.

This type of Skills Development Plan is different from a Performance Improvement Plan, which is focused on improving or developing a skill that is lacking and is required for the employee's current role. In this instance, the employee is not meeting the requirements of the job and must improve to remain in the current role. The timeframe for this plan is often 30, 60, or 90 days, and lack of improvement could result in disciplinary action, up to and including dismissal from the job.

*NOTE: *The difference between a **Skills Development Plan** and a **Performance Improvement Plan**. A Skills Development Plan is focused on an employee acquiring a skill or experience that advances or broadens their career, and it may span six months to a year or more. A Performance Improvement Plan is focused on an employee developing or improving a skill required for their current role,* *and it may span 30-90 days. In short, one has a long-term, career advancement focus, and one has a short-term performance improvement focus.*

...

Now, let's get back to sponsorships. Whether you're working within a formal or informal sponsorship structure, the next step is to determine WIFM—What's In It For Me—as it relates to employees and sponsors. It's critical to outline the benefits for each because you'll be "pitching" both groups to get involved.

Depending on your relationship with a potential sponsor, he or she may be intrinsically interested in supporting others because that is just the way he or she is wired. Seek out these people first. They are typically the ones who are the most willing to get started and the most apt to follow through with action after a discussion. They may also be some of the busiest people you know. Don't let that deter you. They'll let you know if the timing isn't right for them, and at the very least you've opened the door for a future discussion.

Identifying potential sponsors for your employees is a continual process. It's also important to tell employees that they should be looking for and approaching potential sponsors as well. This is something that takes a village and employees may have multiple sponsors throughout their career, especially as they move from one department to another or one company to another.

As you serve on various project teams, boards and committees, view other members as potential sponsors and take the time to learn about their background, experiences and leadership style. When approaching potential sponsors, identify the employee(s) you're recommending and make the "ask," which can be as simple as, "Would you consider being a sponsor for _____?"

This is a critical step that is often overlooked. Ask specifically if the leader would consider being a sponsor for your employee. If so, provide background on the employee, their key accomplishments and potential jobs or assignments where you see a good fit. This is also a time to highlight their transferable skills, like communication, collaboration and project management, per our discussion in Chapter 1. This is especially true if you're looking for a "stretch assignment" beyond an employee's current functional area, and you can help the sponsor "connect the dots" between the employee's skill set and the sponsors' potential positions.

Sponsorship Needs Awareness

Now that we've outlined a process or series of steps we can take as leaders, let's take a look at the need from an employee perspective. When employees ask for sponsorship, they're looking for leaders to do three things:

- Share my potential with your peers.
- Recommend me for succession planning.
- Talk to me about where and how you recommend me and why.

Let's look at each one of these in more detail.

SHARE MY POTENTIAL WITH YOUR PEERS

One ideal place for sharing an employee's potential with your peers is during quarterly or annual team reviews with your fellow leadership team. These meetings are often a combination of discussions about employees' accomplishments, and corresponding compensation so some of this conversation about employees' skillsets happens naturally.

Another group setting that lends itself well to advocating for employees is an annual leadership summit or off-site conference where global leaders gather, often to discuss short-term and long-term goals for the business. Networking time is frequently built into the agenda and scheduling a coffee chat with another leader or group of leaders or even connecting informally can easily be done in this setting. And leaders who are thinking about upcoming goals are also thinking about the teams they will need to accomplish those goals, so succession planning or team building is often top of mind.

As leaders are thinking about current and future needs for their teams, one question to ask a leader or a potential sponsor is, "What skills do you have and what skills do you need on your team?" This can help direct the discussion to a skills-based dialog and then you can evaluate if you have an employee with the skillset the leader needs or not.

When I worked at Purina, Neal Lewis often talked to his leaders about the team building process and how critical it was, beginning with recruiting and selection. He would even identify specific skills among his own leadership team and then explain why we were each chosen and the value we each added. Not only was this a validation and recognition of individual talent, it spoke to the power of the collective team.

He also directed us to do the same thing with our respective teams and even coached us to "hire your weakness." This seems counter intuitive at first, but he went on to explain that my strong marketing and communication skills were his "weakness" and his strong finance and information systems skills were my weakness. Together we each used our strengths to excel individually and collectively as a team. He would often remind us, "If you were all just alike, I'd only need one of you. I need ALL of you." What a great example that was for me as a young leader.

If the group setting isn't the best approach for your leadership team, another avenue is a 1:1 meeting or call with key leaders within your group or in other functional areas. If you think your employee would benefit from a "rotation" or "special assignment" in another area, meet with the leader of that group to discuss the possibilities.

This is another opportunity to connect with HR. They may have a structure for rotational assignments within or among various departments. They may also be aware of groups or individual leaders who are short-staffed and could use additional short-term assistance via "special assignment."

Sometimes a special assignment can be covering for a family leave or it can be a job share situation or short-term coverage in the field when additional employees are needed to service a large customer or support a new project with a quick turn-around time. These assignments can be a "win/win" for the leader who needs help and the employee who needs experience. We'll touch on this more in Chapter 9 as we learn about another Rock Star Millennial who continued to advance his career by "raising his hand" for special projects.

RECOMMEND ME FOR SUCCESSION PLANNING

Although it's preferable to separate succession planning meetings from annual employee performance review meetings, sometimes they occur together, especially if the leadership team is global and has limited face-to-face interactions.

Depending on the size of the team and the depth of the bench strength, leaders may be planning to backfill positions in as little as 6-12 months or as long as three to five years. Given the structure of the organization, they may also have a "tiered approach" where they're planning for short-term and long-term openings and identifying potential employees to fill key roles.

It's not unusual for a high-performing employee to be considered as a successor for multiple roles, especially if they have demonstrated an aptitude for flexibility and a willingness to learn. In this case, it's the leader's role to not "over commit" the employee for multiple roles simultaneously but rather look at various roles in succession and the skills required for each position.

Sponsors can play a key role here if they know the employee well enough to speak to their "track record" and can site examples of specific performance or a collection of unique experiences. Here's an example.

When I was the project manager for building the Caterpillar Visitors Center, Linda Kraftzenk was my boss, but she also was my sponsor. My role was to build the facility over a two-year period and then turn it over to the facility manager, who was yet to be named. Linda was a true servant leader who took the time to get to know me and to learn about my background. Because she had done her homework, Linda knew I had a collection of unique experiences including: leadership and culture development, dealer marketing, factory tours, facility communications, media and public relations, tourism, event planning, and training.

I later found out that she had developed "an elevator speech" about my diverse background that explained how I was uniquely qualified to manage the center once it was opened. She talked to her peers and her leaders at multiple levels about

Linda Kraftzenk was my boss and my sponsor and a frequent visitor to the trailer and job site when we were building the Caterpillar Visitors Center.

my skillset over the next two years, and I was ultimately offered the manager role, thanks in large part to Linda's persistent advocacy, knowledge sharing and support. She was indeed a leader and sponsor extraordinaire.

TALK TO ME ABOUT WHERE AND HOW YOU RECOMMEND ME AND WHY

While leadership meetings are confidential, and it's not appropriate to share verbatim comments with employees, you can let them know that they are highly thought of by the leadership team and give them a sense of the future positions they're being considered for and the corresponding skills required. This discussion is the natural prelude to creating a Skills Development Plan for them, making sure to connect the dots between the skills they need to develop and the future opportunities.

You can also share the role you played in the leadership team discussion and let your employee know how you advocated on their behalf and why. Let them know the potential you see in them and the confidence you have in them to take on these future roles. Identify their accomplishments that you shared with the larger leadership team and recognize the values they've demonstrated like integrity, work ethic, creativity or knowledge sharing. Let them know what specifically you value about them and why they are important to the team and to you.

In addition to your advocacy, let your employees know when other leaders inquire about them and how you responded. I learned from one of my Caterpillar leaders how to do this well. She was focused on broadening my career but in a strategic way. As other leaders would call her and inquire about my availability or a possible "move date," she would review the open position and evaluate the perspective role and leader. Then we would talk about if and how the role might expand my skills and fit in my career path. Together we would make a decision, and she would respond to her peer on my behalf. Each time I felt informed and valued because she had involved me in the discussion. More importantly, she gave me a role model to replicate with others.

This transparency is key with your employees. They want to know about these conversations and be part of them whenever possible. They want to know if other leaders are asking about them and want to know what you are saying on their behalf. Many of you may be having these conversations with peers but not sharing the information with employees because it was determined that they weren't the right fit or it wasn't the right time. Talk to them anyway. Your transparency and their involvement are just as important, if not more important, than the result. The other positive here is your employees are learning from you how to do this well when they become leaders.

As a leader, it's also important to communicate to employees that sometimes a plan comes together and sometimes another plan evolves. Let them know the experience they're gaining may come into play with another opportunity—one that isn't even on their radar or a position that doesn't even exist yet.

When I think back on my experience with the Caterpillar Visitors Center, all of those diverse experiences I had acquired prior to becoming the manager weren't part of a grand plan. I had taken opportunities in different areas of interest and taken on special assignments like project managing the building of the center. All of those culminated in an opportunity that didn't exist when I was doing career planning with my boss five years earlier. This is where preparation and opportunity come together. Our job as leaders is to prepare employees with a diverse skillset so when an opportunity does arise, they are well qualified to be considered.

In short, our employees are asking us to sponsor them, support them in succession planning and share our discussions with them on both of these fronts.

We'll talk more in Chapter 5 about continuing the dialog with employees and extending that support beyond career planning as we look at the best ways to work with them in various locations, with multiple technologies and alternative schedules.

PART II

WHAT MILLENNIALS WANT FROM THEIR COMPANY

TO THIS POINT, WE'VE TALKED about what millennials want from their leaders, which includes some things like clear expectations, on-going feedback, mentoring, sponsorship and leadership development. In this part, we'll take a look at what employees want from their company, why these things are important to them, and how you as leaders can have an impact.

CORRIE HECK SCOTT

Corrie Heck Scott,
Director Global
Communications
for Food & Water
Sustainability at The
Nature Conservancy

CORRIE HECK SCOTT is the Director of Global Communications for Food & Water Sustainability at The Nature Conservancy (TNC). Corrie is a Rock Star Millennial, and she summarized what millennials want from a company in two simple words: transparency and connectivity.

"I don't need to know everything about my leader's daily life, but I want to understand who they are as a person," she said. "One of the coolest things about TNC is we have a lot of fun, both personally and professionally. There is such a personal connection here, and there is value placed on having a deeper understanding of who people are."

So how does Corrie's passion for sustainability align with her work? "This is my dream job! It's an amazing combination of things I'm good at and things I'm motivated by. I wanted a global position so I could work at scale. It's also deeply personal because it's at the core of what we all put in our bodies. This job is about telling the right story and getting that story in front of the right people at the right time.

"This job is a professional extension of who I am as a person and how I find my purpose. I live on our family farm so when I walk out of my home office from my day job, focused on global food and water security, I move to my evening job on my own farm where I'm planting cover crops and capturing rain water to grow food that feeds my family," she said.

Why is that important? Corrie and her husband Kenji are raising their children—Henry, 3, and Avery, 7 months—and instilling a set of values in the next generation. "As I'm raising my family on the farm that raised my grandfather, I hope we are teaching them to value the right things in the right place and raising them with global perspective, paired with local effort" Corrie added.

Prior to her work at TNC, Corrie's career journey took her from the Chief Communications Officer for the Governor of Hawaii to the Executive Director and Co-Founder of a non-profit called Friends of Hawaii Robotics. She then went on to become a partner in a marketing firm before joining Eureka College (President Reagan's alma mater) as the Director of Marketing & Communications and then moving on to Caterpillar, where she was the Sustainability Communications Manager and later Media Relations & Public Affairs Manager.

As she thought about her greatest challenges and accomplishments, Corrie found they went hand in hand. "My greatest challenge is narrowing my scope. I want to take on the world and solve the world's problems. I tend to see the big picture with both the immediate project ahead of me and the next 10 steps after that, so my challenge is to see the whole scope but carve out the sliver I can impact- and most importantly- remind myself that handling my sliver well is the priority."

Her greatest accomplishment? "Putting parameters around my work. I'm not willing to give away my personal life to get it all done now, and I don't feel guilty any more about earning a good salary but not working every waking moment. I used to be a workaholic, and now I understand that the value I'm bringing during those work hours is what they're paying me for. TNC has a stated 35-hour work week, and I'm averaging 42 hours, which is half what I've worked other places. I'm so much more focused and productive, and I know my work is making a difference in making the world better. And that's important to me."

CHAPTER 5

BE COMFORTABLE WITH FLEXIBLE SCHEDULES AND LOCATIONS

AS LEADERS IF YOU'RE ACCUSTOMED to managing small, local teams and used to predominantly face-to-face interaction, becoming comfortable with remote workers, flexible schedules and multiple locations can be a tough hill to climb.

At Caterpillar, I was privileged to lead global teams at different times throughout my career and subsequently learned, as a matter of survival, how to build teams and develop relationships with employees I'd never met in person.

One of my biggest learnings from those opportunities, which has been reinforced in mentoring millennials, is that regardless of where your employees sit, getting to know them personally and learning how they like to be recognized and rewarded are good conversation starters. Think back to the "Getting to Know You" questions from Chapter 3 and the process of building trust through the "touchpoints" discussion from Chapter 2. Both of these topics apply and may be even more important with remote workers.

Sometimes it's easier to get started with processes or protocols that are already familiar, like having regular 1:1 meetings with your direct reports. Using a mobile phone and incorporating digital apps like Facetime or DUO at the very least keeps you connected visually so you're in tune with your employee's non-verbal communication as well as the words you hear them saying.

I also found it helpful to schedule the 1:1s during the employee's core work hours and time zone, which meant I would have calls with Europe early in the day and calls with Asia and India in the evening. I met them on their time zone instead of requesting they change their schedule to accommodate my time zone, even though I was their leader. This small gesture seemed to go a long way in building relationships abroad, and I applied the same thinking with working parents who liked to chat during their commute to or from work.

Conducting staff meetings is a little trickier as connectivity can vary from country to country but using virtual technologies like WhatsApp, ZOOM, TEAMS, Skype or Go To Meeting are popular alternatives for getting the group together so they feel "connected" as a team, which is critical. Building in time at the beginning of these meeting for "greetings" and personal updates or celebrations is also key to building cohesive teams and keeping people connected personally from a distance – which is seen to be consistent and critical to the millennial generation worldwide

One millennial leader who has mastered building teams remotely is Amber Kienast, the Marketing Manager at Renewal by Andersen of Central Illinois and Quad Cities. Let's see what we can learn from this Rock Star Millennial.

AMBER KIENAST

AS THE MARKETING MANAGER, AMBER manages teams in Illinois and Iowa and has responsibility for Proximity Marketing, Events, Retail, and the Customer Call Center. She also has a photography and graphic design background, so she creates all the traditional and non-traditional marketing and advertising pieces for the company, as well as manages social media. Her dream was to lead the marketing efforts at various locations as the owner, Sam Heer, expanded his business. When he opened his Iowa location, she had her first opportunity.

Amber Kienast, is the Marketing Manager at Renewal by Andersen of Central Illinois and Quad Cities

Her goals were two-fold: increase revenue by generating leads in the new territory and reduce costs by bringing an out-sourced customer call center in-house to serve both locations. Amber began by replicating her three marketing teams in the new territory. She recruited and trained team leads and worked with them to develop their own teams for the various marketing divisions, including:

1. **Proximity Marketing** - *canvassers who go door-to-door to meet homeowners*

2. **Events** - *teams that staff booths at trade shows, community gatherings and festivals*

3. **Retail** - *teams that staff informational kiosks in malls, big box and hardware stores and home improvement centers*

After she had her teams in place, she set monthly goals for lead generation and was well on her way to meeting those goals. One of her biggest challenges was building relationships and developing teams from a distance. Amber lived between the two Renewal locations, worked remotely from home and traveled to the offices regularly to touch base with team members. Because most of her meetings were conducted via Facetime and her teams were working evenings and weekends, she was diligent about "touchpoints," even at odd hours. She consistently conducted 1:1 meetings with her leaders and encouraged team members via text, emails and regular phone calls. She recalls these touchpoints made a difference in keeping her teams motivated and led to their success.

Amber's second goal of creating an in-house Customer Call Center to reduce costs was more daunting because she didn't have a team or processes to replicate. She was starting from scratch. From Amber's perspective, she remembers, "I was stuck. I had the vision for the call center but I needed someone to bounce ideas off of and someone who would ask the hard questions and push me. For me, having a mentor helped me put the pedal to the metal. As I made progress week by week, I started to think, 'this is totally doable.'"

At one point, Amber had the realization, "It was me holding myself back. The workload was comparable whether the center was in-house or remote. I had to analyze the feedback and provide leadership for next steps either way, so I was already doing the work. Once I realized this, I had the confidence to move forward, and then we were off and running." Amber met her goal of opening the call center on deadline, recruited and trained the staff and allowed the company to start generating its own leads, which was an annual, large-scale cost avoidance for the business. She also had her first child as the call center was opening and recalled feeling like she gave birth twice that month—a Rock Star Millennial indeed!

Building cohesive teams, staying connected with employees, and making sure you're informed about project work or progress toward goals are areas of focus for leaders. What's the focus for today's millennial employees? Three things, including:

- Encourage working remotely and alternative schedules.
- Focus on quality and quantity of work versus hours worked.
- Honor personal time so we're not connected 24 x 7.

Although these are intrinsically connected, let's look at each one individually and think about ways to make them work for you as leaders, for team members, and for the business.

ENCOURAGE WORKING REMOTELY AND ALTERNATIVE SCHEDULES

Supporting employees who are working remotely and are on alternative schedules is important for young employees today. This is more accepted in some industries, businesses, or segments than others. For example, when I led the media team at Caterpillar, we had folks all over the world who worked in various locations and different time zones, and we all worked remotely at various times. That was the nature of the job before it was popular.

When I managed the Executive Office (EO) communicators, I found that each communicator's schedule could vary depending on the travel schedule or location of the Executive Office member(s) he or she was supporting. So for them and their jobs, working remotely was a necessity and even planning team meetings was sometimes just not possible because of the disparate schedules.

When I managed the Caterpillar Visitors Center, we were constantly hosting busloads of Caterpillar dealers, customers, fans and school children, so there was no opportunity to work remotely. We were giving tours and hosting events at the center and needed everyone to be physically present to do their job. Cross-training was essential to support others who might be overloaded. The same was true of the factory tour teams who were part of Visitor Services. Although these groups – EO Communications, Caterpillar Visitors Center, and Visitor Services tours– were all within the same company, the possibility of working remotely was driven by the needs of the business and could work well for some positions and not others.

How is it with the team you lead? Is it more convenient to have them assembled on site or is it required? Is it possible to have a hybrid of team members working remotely some days and on-site other days? Could you have "core hours" of 9am-2pm when you ask employees to be on site and then allow flexible schedules on either side of those hours?

I often had young moms on my teams who chose to work from home early in the morning before their children were up, which could be 4am-6am. Then they would get their children ready for school or daycare and work 9am-3 or 4pm in the office. After they finished dinner and the evening activities with their families, they would often sign on again at 8 or 9pm to tie up any loose ends. For some, this worked well, and they were happy with the flexibility and glad not to be scrutinized for their limited "on-site" office hours.

I was very accommodating because I knew what this felt like and remembered having the anxiety of needing to leave by 5:05pm to be on time to pick up children in two places by 5:30pm. It was stressful every day. I felt like I was neglecting my work by not staying to finish everything completely, yet I didn't want to be late to pick up my children and cut short our evening time together.

When my children were young, we didn't have laptops and cell phones (I know! Hard to believe.) and the office hours of 8am-5pm were required. If I couldn't get everything done in the 45 hours I had at the office, I remember going to work on Saturday mornings from 5-8am, while my boys were still sleeping. My husband owned a business that was open on Saturdays and I needed to be home by 8:15 so my husband could go to work. That schedule worked for us for three years and allowed each of us to stay on top of our workload and still care for our young boys.

As you work with your team to meet their needs, your needs and the needs of the business, two things to keep in mind are flexibility and attitude. Your ability to be flexible on a day or period of time when your employee needs it most can pay big dividends in terms of their loyalty and discretionary effort going forward. The other "trust builder" is approaching them first, instead of waiting until they come to you with the "ask." If you recognize the schedule challenges in your millennial workforce and they are not asking for flexibility but may benefit from it, consider surfacing the idea with them. I learned that lesson the hard way. Here's how:

Neal Lewis taught me so many leadership lessons during my time at Purina, but this one fundamentally changed me as a person and as a leader. When I became one of his direct reports, I was part of his weekly leadership meetings. He often gave us assignments for the week, and one Monday he said our assignment would be to know three personal things about everyone who worked for us. The caveat was it couldn't be information from their personnel folder.

As a young Lousy Leader, I asked where we would find that information if we couldn't use the folders, and he said very wisely, "You need to TALK to them." It seems silly now but at the time that was just an overwhelming task, and I may have had 10 people on my team. Boy, did I have a lot to learn.

All we knew was that he would stop us at some point that week to ask what we'd learned. The trick was we wouldn't know when he was going to ask us or which employee he would ask about, so we had to know three personal things about ALL of them as soon as possible. The Type-A personality in me blocked time on my calendar and "interviewed" each of my team members until I felt like I was prepared.

Sure enough, I saw Neal in the hall one day that week, and he asked me to walk with him to his next meeting. On the way, he said "Tell me three personal things about Kathy on your team." I told him she was recently divorced, had an 18-month-old baby and was in the process of moving to a new apartment.

"Good," he said, and then asked, "What have you done to help her?" Honest to goodness, I looked him straight in the eye and said, "That wasn't part of the assignment."

I was such a Lousy Leader at that time he should have fired me about three times a day. Eventually, I recovered from the shock of the follow-up question and said, "I did help her. I changed her hours. Her new apartment is farther from the office, so now she's coming in at 8:30 instead of 8:00 o'clock, and she'll work until 5:00." For a moment I thought I had passed the test...until Neal asked the pivotal question, "Did you go to her or did she come to you?" I quickly responded," She came to me but I said it was ok."

Neal shook his head and said, "Kathryn, know your people. If you don't know your people, you don't know what they need. If you don't know what they need, you can't help them. And if you can't help them, what in the WORLD are you doing here?" Before I could respond he added, "As leaders, we're here to serve, and if you're not here to serve, you need to step out." I became a different leader that day: one who chose to lead by serving.

The lesson I learned was simple – part of serving was becoming a proactive leader. Just as I focused on anticipating my boss's needs or my customer's needs and acting before they asked, I realized that same anticipation and proactive action was of great value to employees. I was amazed at the difference it made when I approached employees with an alternative before they even asked. The end result was the same. In the case of Kathy, I changed her hours when she asked me. But I missed out on the residual "good will" and loyalty I could have garnered from that same situation by anticipating her need and approaching her first.

Once I learned this lesson, I made it a practice to approach employees about taking "comp time" or planning vacations or creating a flexible work schedule before they asked "permission." I remember what this felt like as an employee and knew how stressful it was to ask for "special dispensation" from a boss. I also knew what it felt like to develop "divergent" behavior to cover for personal schedules in lieu of transparency. Here's an example.

When my boys were in grade school, I had a great boss at Caterpillar who was also a working mom and was proactive with me about my schedule. Lois Boaz was one of the few women leaders at Caterpillar at the time, and I sought out a position on her team, partially because of her leadership style and flexibility.

She knew I had young children, and during one of our first meetings she said, "Don't ever let me make you late to pick up your children and don't ever miss the activities you want to attend because of work. Let me know what's important to you, and we'll be careful how we put it on your calendar, so you don't have to explain it to anyone."

I was grateful for her flexibility and her generosity in valuing my priorities. I was careful not to take advantage of the situation and assured her I would get my work done and work additional hours as needed to compensate for the time I took off.

When she asked about my priorities, I told her I wanted to be a room mother, participate in my boys' seasonal parties and also attend chapel periodically if they had a special role. She thought all of that was do-able and counseled me to use a code on my work calendar instead of identifying the time as "room mother or chapel." I told her I would use the initials "CLS" which stood for Concordia Lutheran School. That way she would know where I was and could help me "protect" that time.

I continued that practice for a few years, thinking no one had really noticed, but I found out differently. As I was leaving that role to move on to become the Global Marketing Manager for Caterpillar Logistics Services (CLS), my team gave a little going-away celebration and invited different leaders to say a few kind words. One leader thanked me for my service and said he was surprised to see me leave and go to work for the Logistics group. Another leader promptly spoke up and said he wasn't surprised at all since he knew from my calendar that I had been going to meetings at CLS for the past four years.

My boss and I got a good chuckle out of that one, but I also learned another leadership lesson. Going forward, I made it a point to encourage my teams to take time for their children's activities and schedule them on their calendar just as she had done for me. Looking back this seems like a small step, but at the time it was HUGE!

So what can we take away from these examples? As a leader, when you approach your employees first, your actions speak volumes. You're saying that you trust them and value them – and this is not just for young moms, but young dads and all other employees with or without children. You're also saying that you not only tolerate this flexibility but you're encouraging it, acting as their advocate. Each time I used this approach, I saw employees respond with gratitude and sometimes even relief that I truly knew them and understood their needs. This simple gesture was impactful as a trust milestone and a leadership example to model. Lesson learned.

FOCUS ON QUALITY AND QUANTITY OF WORK VERSUS HOURS WORKED

For many leaders, focusing on the quality and quantity of work versus the hours worked can be a mindset shift, especially if their experiences were with in-office mandatory times. As more and more employees work flexible hours and work from remote locations, the number of hours worked is harder for leaders to quantify and less important, unless employees are in a "billable hours" situation. As leaders, empowering remote employees to be successful begins with setting clear expectations and creating measurable goals with specific timelines, as we discussed in Chapter 2. This is particularly important to today's millennial employees, as is reinforcing the value of those deliverables and the part they play in reaching departmental goals and the company's success. (Refer to the **Shared Goals** document highlighted in Chapter 2 and illustrated in the Tools section in the back of the book.)

Sophie Wade is the President of the NYC chapter of the National Association of Women Business Owners and author of the book *Embracing Progress*. She is recognized as an authority on "Future-of-Work" issues and regularly writes articles on this subject for *HUFF POST*. In a recent article entitled, "The Six Secrets of Effective Remote Working and Collaborating," Sophie shared the success SAP® has had with measuring results. "They produce Total Economic Impact reports for themselves and customers to confirm the purpose of the collaboration and track its impact and successful completion." [1]

Fuze is one of SAP's clients, and Colin Doherty is the CEO of Fuze. He "recently made the decision for the company to go virtual and no longer have a central headquarters in favor of regional hubs," Sophie reported. "Doherty himself is passionate about productivity, not attendance, which is another essential shift with a distributed workforce," she explained. In addition, "Focusing on outcomes to assess progress ensure(s) an equitable evaluation of all employees' performance," she continued.

Working with teams to compartmentalize the specific work each member is responsible for is part of the tracking and accountability. This also provides data and logic for workload balancing among individuals and teams as change occurs and teams evolve.

HONOR PERSONAL TIME SO WE'RE NOT CONNECTED 24 X 7

Honoring personal time for today's millennial employees is high on their request list. Depending on the employee and their job, some guard their personal time well, especially if they've been working for a few years. Others who are just beginning their careers may be so focused on doing a good job and wanting to be promoted that they need to be reminded to take time to rejuvenate and unplug.

Given current technology, some employees are literally connected to their work 24 x 7 and often have a hard time unplugging, which adds to their stress level, leads to burn out and contributes to lower productivity. All of these things contribute to unhappy employees and high turnover.

Another Sophie Wade article that addresses this issue is entitled, "Productivity And Performance With A Distributed Workforce: Control, Choice, And Communication." She acknowledges that "one challenging aspect of the new technology-enhanced working environment is the disappearance of traditional boundaries. This is often exacerbated when someone is not working in the office—with even more blurred definitions of office/home, work/leisure, etc."[2]

She adds that boundaries such as "no emails after hours" are tough to mandate and encourages leaders to have the honest discussion with their team members, asking them:

- "What does a good work style look like to you?"
- "What does staying connected mean to you and your team?"
- "What does it mean to be connected or disconnected after hours or on vacation?"

These questions are extensions of the ones we talked about in Chapter 3 as part of the "Getting To Know You" dialog. It might make sense to add these questions to that list during your introductory conversation with a new employee or add them into a 1:1 discussion as your employee gets more involved in project work. The important thing is to make sure these questions are asked and answered for each employee. Why? Because sometimes we're not tuned into the signals our employees are sending us and vice versa. Here's an example.

When I managed the Caterpillar Visitors Center, we had two shifts working six days a week, which included maintenance, housekeeping, catering and visitor services staffs. In addition, we had security personnel on site for three shifts, seven days a week. We rented meeting rooms from 7am-5pm Monday through Friday and were open to the public and conducted tours from 10am to 5pm Monday through Saturday. Our evening events ran any day of the week, usually from 5 or 6pm until 10pm, except children's birthday parties, which we hosted during two shifts on Saturdays. The staff numbered 52 people including employees, retirees, and contract workers.

Some folks were working standard shifts and 40-hour weeks. Others were working day and night for 80 hours a week. Because of the multiple shifts, different payrolls and varying needs of the business, some employees were cross trained and could fill in for one another while others could not. I also noticed some employees responding to my emails at all hours of the day and night, which told me they were constantly connected and not getting a break. It didn't take long for the high-performing employees to get sick, start calling off their shifts and show signs of burnout. Looking back, I should have seen this coming, but I didn't.

By the time I realized what was happening, we had already lost some good employees who left with a sour taste in their mouth. Understandable. At that point, I started working with each supervisor to make sure workloads were more balanced, hourly employees were getting overtime pay or additional time off where earned, and salaried employees were given "comp time" to use at their discretion in recognition of the long hours worked during a given week. I also applied the "proactive leadership" approach of thanking employees ahead of time when they were scheduled to work extra-long hours and asking them when they would like to schedule comp time before they even requested it.

Another lesson learned from this experience was this: Sometimes it's best to say things out loud and in writing, repeatedly, so that your team knows you're serious. During our stand-up meetings at the beginning of each shift, I began telling employees if I had an urgent need I would call or text them, and I pledged to keep that to a minimum. I even started writing in the subject line of emails: "PLEASE DO NOT RESPOND TO THIS EMAIL UNTIL YOU'RE BACK IN THE OFFICE." I got some humorous notes along the way, but in time they understood I truly meant what I said, and there was no need to be connected to email 24 x 7. Today, you can also schedule delayed delivery so your emails arrive during work hours for your employees. Either way, the end result is a happier and more productive staff, and the modified schedules are more sustainable.

So far, we've looked closely at several things employees want from their boss, ranging from support in navigating their careers to giving honest feedback to coaching and sponsoring them for development. As we move into Chapter 6, we'll look at what today's employees want from a company beyond salary and benefits, and why things like personal and company values and community involvement matter to them.

CHAPTER 6

DEMONSTRATE STRONG VALUES & PROVIDE BENEFIT OPTIONS

TODAY'S EMPLOYEES WANT to be part of something bigger. They want to know that their work matters, and they want to see how the work they do contributes to the greater good. While employees may take pride in the products a company produces or the quality of services a company offers, the real emotional connection comes when employees "feel" like they're involved in furthering a company's purpose and making the world a better place.

Deloitte's recent "Global Millennial Survey" concluded that millennials "expect businesses to enhance lives and provide livelihoods." They look to businesses to "balance profit with protecting the planet and helping to solve society's most challenging problems." In addition, they want to see companies "demonstrate internally and externally what they are doing to make the world a better place."[1]

Chris Tuff echoes these comments in his book, *The Millennial Whisperer*. He writes, "Millennials are eager to give their best for purpose-driven companies and will work hard to make us profitable if they first know the purpose behind the work." He goes on to say, "This generation is incredibly focused on leaving a mark on society. They'll give us much more when they believe we're not *only* looking out for our bottom line."[2]

I saw this firsthand at Purina as the company lived out its purpose of developing people and enriching lives by uniting would-be pet owners with foster pet programs and engaging seniors with companion pets. They also involved employees in their product development process by encouraging us to be "taste testers" at work by sampling different grocery products and giving our input on anything from Hostess Twinkies and Ding Dongs to Chex Mix flavors. We could also include our families as taste testers by taking home samples of baby food and children's cereals for our children to taste so we could provide feedback. In the same way, they provided pet food and treats for our pets to sample and evaluate – which, in our case, was slightly more challenging because we had Labradors who would eat ANYTHING and act like they loved it!

At Caterpillar, employees were each given a number of paid volunteer hours a year that they could spend during their workday to support an organization of their choice. The company also worked with community leaders around the world to organize employee involvement in Junior Achievement and Reading Buddy school programs, Habitat for Humanity home construction teams, river cleanup projects and Earth Day tree planting.

Employees often cited the work of The Caterpillar Foundation as a source of pride and engagement. In particular, they noted the Foundation's work with Opportunity International to provide micro loans to women/small businesses in Uganda and the work with Water.org to supply toilets and clean drinking water to communities in developing countries around the world.

When one of our leaders wanted to get us riled up, he was fond of saying to employees, "As long as there are children in the world without food and families without clean drinking water, we have work to do. Because it's *our* customers who use *our* equipment to build the roads and bridges that connect these people to a better way of life." You could see employees physically stand taller and walk away energized, knowing they had a part to play in building a better world.

What can we learn from these examples? As leaders, we too have a role to play here in sharing the good work our company does and connecting employees to that work. In short, employees are looking for three things from their company, and you can play a role in facilitating each of these:

- Tell me what values are important to the company and to you and why.
- Share the company's community involvement and why it's important.
- Talk to me about benefit options and reward packages that can impact me personally.

Now, let's look at each one of these in a little more detail. As leaders, you're the first and most trusted line of communication for your employees; sharing your personal perspectives on the company and its positive impact can be inspiring for them and rejuvenating for you.

TELL ME WHAT VALUES ARE IMPORTANT TO THE COMPANY AND WHY

Whether your company has well-documented values with corresponding communications, learning and recognition elements or your company's values are less formal and passed on via story-telling and urban legends, values are important to this generation. Your connection to them is also important.

From a millennial perspective, three words to remember and use frequently are "and here's why." In this case, they want to understand how the company's values relate to what the company does and how you as a leader connect with them. The conversation they're looking for here goes beyond corporate speak— they're looking for something personal and authentic. Here's an example of one leader's experience and how his honesty with employees was a turning point.

The *"Our Common Values"* Transformation

Before I went to work for Caterpillar, I worked for Converse Marketing, a marketing consulting firm owned by Jane Converse that did a lot of work with multiple divisions of Caterpillar. One of our clients was Jim Despain, who was the Vice President of the Track-Type Tractor Division. Jim enlisted Converse Marketing to collaborate with him and his leadership team on something that ultimately became a culture-change journey for his division and included the creation of "Our Common Values."

The protocol at Converse Marketing was to begin client meetings with the question, "What business problems do we want to solve?" The answer to this question directed our research, which was always the first step, and the research findings led to a business plan. In this case, the business problems we were solving were reducing costs and employee attrition, both of which were measurable and time sensitive.

The journey that resulted in positive business results and happier, more productive employees is chronicled in the book, *...And Dignity for All— Unlocking Greatness with Values-Based Leadership,* authored by Jim Despain and Jane Converse. The short story is this: identifying values by which leaders and employees would live and work, defining the corresponding behaviors behind those values and holding each other accountable were the keys to success. [3]

The nine values that ultimately comprised *Our Common Values* were: Trust, Mutual Respect, Teamwork, Empowerment, Risk Taking, Sense of Urgency, Continuous Improvement, Commitment and Customer Satisfaction. It's been argued that having nine values was way too many, but Jim explained in his book how the values interacted and why each was important.

"Nine building blocks interact to form the structure of *Our Common Values*. Trust and Mutual Respect are the strong foundation and starting point. Teamwork, Empowerment, Risk Taking and a Sense of Urgency rise out of them and give support to Continuous Improvement and Commitment. Customer Satisfaction is the peak," he wrote.

"All the values are critical to success," he continued. "If any value is absent, the structure is unstable and incomplete. *Our Common Values* structure is a fragile balance that depends on all people. Interaction is its strength." He also emphasized that Trust was the cornerstone and without it the structure couldn't stand. To further illustrate his point, when he appeared in person, Jim often used nine wooden building blocks to build the *Our Common Values* structure and then he would pull out the cornerstone of Trust and watch the structure collapse—every time.

In order to bring all the values to life, employees were asked to define the values in their own words, and their words were used in communication and learning materials. Once behaviors were defined, holding people accountable for their behavior was next—beginning at the top.

Jim shared his personal leadership journey with employees as he explained in the book. "I began a meaningful introspection. The question I struggled with was whether or not I could change and live up to the standards we would be requiring of others. I knew I had to change. I knew the worst thing that could happen was for me to introduce the values process to the organization and then not be able to walk the talk. Fortunately, I wanted to change and was determined. I wanted to be the kind of leader our vision required," he shared in the book

And change he did. He embraced the values and changed his leadership style from an autocratic manager to a true leader. Did he stumble along the way? Yes. Did he admit it when he didn't act like the leader he wanted to be? Yes. Did this inspire others to do the same? Yes. Did the change in leadership style lead a culture change for the employees and a turn-around for the business? Yes.

His example caught fire within the company and led other divisions to create their own values-based cultures. Ultimately the company united on this front and created one set of corporate values that every division adopted. What does this scenario teach us? Be transparent. Be authentic. Be the leader who talks to employees about the company's values and how they have impacted you personally and professionally. In Jim's case, living the values made him a better leader –and he will even say it made him a better person. This change in leadership style impacted other leaders which in turn improved employee engagement, which improved business results. One leader summarized the transformation by saying, "This proves what we know in our hearts: that trusting and respecting people is not only a better way to interact, it makes good business sense."

SHARE THE COMPANY'S COMMUNITY INVOLVEMENT AND WHY IT'S IMPORTANT

One of my favorite roles at Caterpillar was being the Director of Global Sustainability. At Caterpillar, sustainability was defined as a commitment to building a better world and involved a balance of environmental stewardship, social responsibility and economic growth.

My job was to communicate, communicate, communicate – internally with employees and externally with targeted audiences and the general public about the good work Caterpillar, its employees, dealers and customers were doing in the world of sustainability. I often traveled to job sites to see firsthand the work that was being done to restore the environment and use natural infrastructure as part of a rebuilding process.

Millennials around the globe were some of our most ardent allies. They formed sustainability teams in their region or facility and often led projects for recycling, promoted "green" tours and participated in environmental studies. They coordinated Earth Day celebrations and collaborated with other locations to share best practices. You too can easily replicate any of these activities at your company or go to _Companies for Good_ for other ideas and even some help organizing activities for your team.

One area of particular interest for Caterpillar employees was the company's work with the "Natural Infrastructure Initiative." This was a coalition that Caterpillar led in collaboration with The Nature Conservancy, Ducks Unlimited, AE Com, Brown & Root and Great Lakes Dredge and Dock. The group also worked closely with the Army Corp. of Engineers, the World Wildlife Fund and the Wildlife Society.

What role did Caterpillar play? Caterpillar worked with Ducks Unlimited to restore wetlands and grasslands and teamed up with the Army Corps of Engineers to reconstruct navigation channels. The company also collaborated with The Nature Conservancy on the advocacy front to add natural infrastructure language into legislation that was ultimately passed into law.

Why is this important? Each of these actions benefited sustainability in a different way and together they demonstrated Caterpillar's commitment to building a better world, while at the same time impacting the greater good.

Because this work was of such interest to employees, I was often invited to speak at all employee meetings and new employee orientation to share these sustainability stories. If I was part of a panel, we prepared discussion topics and potential audience participation questions, some of which leaders used as discussion starters in their own team meetings.

Whether you share this information via team meetings or during one-one-one discussions with employees, be sure to add your commentary as well. Employees want to know how this work impacts and inspires you—both of which will engage them.

PINK PEARLS OF HOPE

ONE OF MY opportunities to engage employees and talk about how Caterpillar was building a better world touched more lives than I could have ever imagined. Mine included. During my tenure in sustainability, I was invited to be the Caterpillar Ambassador for Susan G. Komen for a year. While this role was voluntary, it was an honor to be asked and to serve as I was celebrating my 10-year anniversary as a breast cancer survivor. Since Peoria, IL is the hometown of Caterpillar and Susan G. Komen, the connection was even more special.

During my time as an ambassador, I shared the story of a quiet network of *Caterpillar employees* all around the world —some of whom were cancer survivors— and took it upon themselves to reach out to other employees who had been diagnosed with cancer and offer to mentor them throughout their journey. I didn't know this informal network existed until I was diagnosed with breast cancer and then my mentor, Marsha Schoenemann, reached out to me.

She asked about my diagnosis and treatment plan and shared her journey with me as well. I thought this was a very generous gesture, but little did I know it was the first of many. After my first chemo treatment she called to see how it had gone. The amazing thing here is, she lived in Singapore! I remember saying, "Marsha, it's 3am in Singapore!" and her response was, "Yep, I can tell time. How was your treatment today and how are you feeling?" We talked for an hour, and she called me after every chemo treatment— for four months. Remarkable.

The next employee who reached out to me was Jan Arnold. She offered to be my "Voice" during the journey and keep friends, family and co-workers updated via calls, emails and Caring Bridge posts on my behalf. She also organized meal and floral deliveries and assembled a team to walk in the Komen Race for the Cure and make donations in my name. Above and beyond.

Megan Parsons also reached out to support me through my journey. She was working in our Beijing, China office, and she made a special effort to visit me while she was on home leave—a visit I'll never forget. She brought me a beautiful set of pink pearls from Beijing and explained they were "Pink Pearls of Hope," a reminder that many people were hoping with me and sending good thoughts for my health and healing. My response was simple and profound. Tears.

I wore the pink pearls often and found they did give me hope. I wished I could share that hope with others, but I didn't know how. Megan did. The next time she came she brought ten more sets of pearls, knowing that when I was well again I would mentor others.

Photo Credit: Scott Spitznagle,
Rock Tail Productions

I became part of that Caterpillar network, reaching out to those who were newly diagnosed and mentoring them along the way. As they celebrated milestones, like undergoing surgery or finishing chemo or radiation, I would pass along Pink Pearls of Hope with a note about the meaning and origin. Before long I had mentored ten women, passed along the pearls and thought my work was done.

But the pearls kept coming. One by one. Sets of pearls would show up on my desk. Randomly. Anonymously. Sometimes a person would stop by my office, pearls in hand and say, "I've heard your story and I want to be part of the journey." Caterpillar people all over the world were buying, shipping or hand carrying pearls for people they didn't know and would never meet but wanted to help.

Just about the time I would be notified of newly diagnosed employees to mentor, another batch of pearls would show up. You might think it was a coincidence if it had happened a time or two, but it continued—not weeks, not months, but years—10 years to be exact. For 10 years, I never ran out of pearls. I believe things happen for a reason, and I knew my purpose was clear.

When my last visitor surprised me with 20 sets of pearls, I asked him to please share the website or name of the shop where he had purchased them so I could start buying them online. What do you suppose the American name of that little shop in Beijing, China, is called? Katherine Pearls.

So what is the message here? Personal connections matter and speaking from the heart matters most. I could truly say that because of the work Caterpillar was doing with Susan G. Komen, people were touched all around the world, and I was a life that was changed.

Photo Credit: Scott Spitznagle, Rock Tail Productions

Peoria Journal Star article: *https://www.pjstar.com/news/20170512/ caterpillar-employee-offers-pink-pearls-of-hope-to-fight-breast-cancer*

Caterpillar Ambassador to Komen video: *https://www.youtube.com/ watch?time_continue=16&v=38EjSFGH2yY&feature=emb_logo*

TALK TO ME ABOUT BENEFIT OPTIONS AND REWARD PACKAGES

While this seems like a fundamental discussion and one that could be handled by HR during employee orientation or annual enrollment for health care, this is another "touchpoint" opportunity for us as leaders with this generation of employees. Many millennials are also struggling with student loan debt and could use direction in the area of finances. While our role is not the one of "coach" in terms of advising employees, we can offer information about what is available, how it can impact them and where else they can go to get more information via a website, workshop or HR professional.

Initiating the discussion as a proactive leader and opening the dialog for any questions is key. Some employees won't want to talk about benefits, but others will—even if they just want to be connected to an additional resource or specialist.

Traditional and Non-Traditional HR Benefits

A conversation starter could be as simple as asking an employee if they are aware the company offers any or all of the following:

- 401K investment opportunity and/or a company match
- Healthcare, pharmaceutical, vision, dental coverage (options)
- Healthcare and childcare Flexible Spending Accounts (FSA)
- On-site or affiliate childcare
- Referrals for elder care and primary caregiver support
- Family Medical Leave options
- Bereavement, vacation, sick days
- Employee Assistance Programs (EAP) for counseling, emotional wellness and substance abuse
- Health club memberships or reimbursements
- On site medical staff, annual physical, flu shots, vaccinations for travel, wellness coaching
- Employee discounts with community partners
- Employee Resource Groups
- Tuition reimbursement
- Mortgage assistance
- Philanthropic contributions and matching programs.

An easy follow up question is asking if they would like any additional information on any of these topics or a referral to someone with specific HR expertise. If your company does email blasts, intranet alerts, webinars or in-home mailers at certain times of the year to promote or further explain these benefits, you can also highlight the timeline and deadlines for employees and encourage them to stay tuned for more information.

While there are likely multiple mediums for communicating and explaining the benefits information, you are an employee's singular and most trusted resource for their rewards programs. These programs could include bonuses, profit sharing, stock distribution or a combination of these. If we think back to Chapter 2, where we talked about setting clear expectations with measurable goals and outlining the corresponding rewards, this is where that groundwork pays off.

This is also where having "progress toward goals" discussions consistently during your employee one-on-one meetings yields dividends and eliminates surprises. In preparation for a rewards discussion, gather the facts, percentages, and payouts ahead of time so you're not doing calculations or find you're missing some critical piece of information once you've started the employee discussion.

Take the time to make a few notes about the employee's specific accomplishments and personal growth so you can comment on their individual progress too. Whether you're leading in a small business that pays monthly or quarterly bonuses or you're leading in a large corporation that gives annual merit increases, the rewards conversation is an important one. Your sincere recognition of the good work that was done and why it matters, is both personal and impactful.

So far, we've taken a close look at what millennials want from their boss and from their company and why those things are important to them. In the next few chapters, we'll look at what they want to learn from your experiences as a leader and how they want to grow and develop in the areas of self-management, personal productivity, self-care and leadership.

PART III

WHAT MILLENNIALS
WANT TO LEARN

THIS GENERATION IS OFTEN CHARACTERIZED as one of "perpetual learners." They thrive on learning new skills, new information and new perspectives. They've grown up in an age where information can be gathered and disseminated instantly at their fingertips. They also seek out others who have experience in something they want to learn or master, particularly in the following four areas:

1. Self-management and personal productivity.
2. Leadership styles that work.
3. Creativity and innovation strategies.
4. Ways we connect and complement.

One of the things these employees do really well is benchmarking others, and as leaders, this is where we have the most to offer. Some of the very fundamentals of self-management, personal productivity and integrating work and home lives that we have learned through the years are the very things they're trying to master. In these next few chapters, we'll look at how best to translate your leadership learnings in a way that is engaging for them and rewarding for you.

CHAPTER 7

SELF-MANAGEMENT AND PERSONAL PRODUCTIVITY

WHEN YOU THINK ABOUT THE areas of self-management or self-care and personal productivity you may have to pause. These are skills you've honed through the years, and you might have to compartmentalize them into specific tasks or tools that work for you. As you take a moment to reflect on your own journey, also consider how to frame your knowledge and life lessons in the three areas that are priorities for millennials:

- Talk to me about self-care, what works for you and why it's important.
- Identify personal productivity tools you've found successful.
- Direct me to self-management, personal productivity resources.

All three are important to this generation. What separates your learning from any research they could do online or through a survey of their peers is you have proven solutions, not theory – and, they can ask you for clarification or follow up real time. You not only know *what* works for you, but you know *how* it works and *why* it works—that's the trifecta! What they're asking is that you share it with them.

TALK TO ME ABOUT SELF-CARE, WHAT WORKS FOR YOU AND WHY IT'S IMPORTANT

When I facilitate workshops or speak on panels, a frequently asked question revolves around managing work and home lives and specifically how to make time for self-care. My response is simple: "Pay yourself first." What does this mean? Make yourself a priority. Set aside some time every day that is just for you. It may only be a few minutes, but make sure it's all yours and you use it to your best advantage. That advantage is different for everyone but the one thing that is consistent is taking the time. You notice I said TAKING. Not wishing. Not asking. TAKING. Here's how I learned that lesson.

When I led the team at the Caterpillar Visitors Center, we were working lots of crazy hours six days a week. Our leadership team was predominantly women, and most were moms. During one of our weekly staff meetings the subject of finding time for yourself came up as a consistent struggle for the women. The men, who were also parents, seemed to do a better job of this so we asked them to share how they found time for themselves. One answered succinctly, "You just take it." The response was utter silence until one brave soul asked, "How?"

The gentleman went on to say he got up early on Sunday mornings to have a couple hours of quiet time to himself while the rest of the family was sleeping. When family members did get up, it was understood by all that this was "Dad's private time" and he was not to be bothered. One of the women quickly replied that such an arrangement would never work at her house, to which he asked, "Have you tried it?" The honest answer was, "No." The suggestion was, "Try it." So she did. She learned that she really didn't need a couple hours once a week, but rather needed 15 minutes in the morning and again in the evening to call her own. Once she "claimed" that time, it became part of her daily ritual, her family's practice and a source of rejuvenation.

Defining And Incorporating Self-Care

Here's the way to bring this into your leadership style and a way to communicate it to your millennial team members. It's really a simple four-step process.

- The first step is being aware of the need to revitalize.
- The second step is identifying what you like to do and understanding which things truly revitalize you.
- The third step is allotting time to do those things that rejuvenate you and making them a priority.
- The last step is incorporating rejuvenation into your daily work life and doing it intentionally as a part of self-care and leadership.

I learned about the power of rejuvenation or revitalization at Purina, and subsequently understood why it was important for me personally and the role it played in leadership, which was a discovery for me. When I was a new supervisor, my boss asked me to identify three things that revitalized me and explain why. Being an overachiever, I identified four things: fresh flowers, handwritten notes or cards, photos of family and friends and a walk outside. His next question was, "*Why* do these things revitalize you?" (which is equally important, if not more important, than knowing what revitalizes you).

I went on to explain fresh flowers reminded me of my grandmother, Nanny, who was a wonderful gardener and always had fresh flowers in her home. Notes and cards from special people in my life and photos of family and friends reminded me of the value of those relationships. A walk outside took me back to nature and reminded me I was part of a bigger world and had a broader purpose.

The next question was, "How can you incorporate those things that revitalize you into your workday?" This was the beginning of my understanding of self-care. From that day forward, I had a vase of fresh flowers on my desk, along with photos and cards, even if they were only a snapshot on my phone. When I was having a tough day, I would take a minute to smell the flowers on my desk, literally, and for that moment I was back in Nanny's garden and it brought me peace.

When I looked at family photos or cards, it reminded me of who really mattered in my life and where I was making a difference and that brought me joy and perspective. I also made time each day to step outside. Some days I walked outside, took a deep breath of fresh air and walked right back inside, but that moment somehow made a difference and gave me renewed energy.

My boss reinforced this leadership lesson for me one morning when he walked by my office, and I was arranging fresh flowers. He smiled, gave me a thumbs up and said, "Good Leader." He recognized I was embarrassed for being "caught" doing this during work hours and he said, "Do you know why I said 'Good Leader'?" When I shook my head, he went on to explain, "Fresh flowers are one of the things that revitalize you, so when I see you taking care of yourself, that's good leadership. The more rejuvenated you are, the more you have to give to your team, your family and to all of us. So keep arranging those flowers, Good Leader."

Asking your employees what revitalizes them and why can be a discussion topic during a 1:1 meeting or it can be one of the "Getting to Know You" questions we talked about in Chapter 3. Your employees may surprise you with the things that revitalize them, like social time or working out or pet care. The way they relax and revitalize may not be the way you revitalize, and that's ok. Just like it was with my boss. I'm pretty sure arranging fresh flowers wasn't on his list of things that revitalized him, but he knew it was important to me. Then he took it one step further. Not only did he indulge me, he encouraged me. The difference here is critical. This is another example of the pro-active leadership style that is equally unexpected and impactful for employees. The contrast between indulging me and encouraging me was profound, and that subtle shift made all the difference.

The same is true for you as a leader. Understanding WHAT revitalizes your employees, the WHY behind it for them and HOW it can be incorporated into their work lives are key learnings. Through your actions, you're teaching them that introspection and self-care are important. You're also modeling a leadership style that sets you apart with millennials. It's one they'll identify as unique. It's one they'll value and talk about with their peers. And because they remember how it felt, it's likely one they'll integrate into their own style and repeat.

Reinforcing Your Words With Actions

The same leader who encouraged me when I demonstrated good self-care also held me accountable when I didn't. Here's how. Part of my marketing communications role at Purina was creating an employee newsletter each month. One month as the deadline approached, I hadn't gotten it done during the week, so I finished the newsletter over the weekend. When I came in Monday morning, I expected my boss to be happy the work was done on time. Instead, he approached me with a stern look and said words I'll never forget, "You are a burden to me."

I felt like I'd been kicked in the stomach. I was so taken aback that it took me a moment to respond. I remember arguing that I was not a "burden." I was his "go-to person" who got things done- just like I did with the newsletter. He went on to explain, "You have two days every week to be home with your husband and your boys. You probably missed half of that time over the weekend doing this newsletter, right? When you do things like this then I worry about you. I worry about your health because you didn't catch up on your sleep or take time to rejuvenate. I worry about your marriage because weekends are a time to reconnect with your spouse. And I worry about your children who didn't get to spend time with their mom this weekend because she was working."

He went on to say, "All of those things are more important to me than this newsletter. Why? Because those are the people who rejuvenate you so you come in to work whole— refreshed and revitalized. As a leader I don't want to carry that burden of making sure you are revitalized. I want you to take charge of that. I want to see you make different choices. I want to see you delegate. I want to see you prioritize. I want to see you put yourself and your family first. That's the leadership I'm looking for from you."

While I realize this type of discussion is highly unlikely in most firms, I call it out because this is exactly the leadership style that will set you apart as a leader. This is the style that communicates you genuinely care about your employees. This authentic caring is what employees will remember. When we gave customer tours at the Caterpillar Visitors Center, we knew our guests wouldn't remember everything we said on the tour, but our goal was that they would remember how we made them feel. Cherished. The same logic applies here. Your employees will remember how you made them feel and, that's precisely the emotional connection that creates engagement and builds loyalty.

So how do you get the conversation started? Share your self-care lessons learned, what's worked well for you and why. Explain how self-care relates to leadership and why it's important. Ask them to do some personal introspection and answer questions for themselves like:

- Who and what revitalizes you and how can you incorporate it into your workday?
- How do you take the time you need daily for self-care and make yourself a priority?
- What are you doing to manage your work and stress in a way that protects your non-work life?

Positive self-talk & affirmations

Another part of self-care that goes hand in hand with revitalizing is learning to monitor and direct self-talk. As I work with millennials, I find there is a lot of interest in this aspect of self-care. In his book, *Smart Talk for Achieving Your Potential,* Lou Tice defines self-talk as "the continual dialogue you have with yourself." Why is this important? "Self-talk is the raw material from which you manufacture your own self-image," Lou explains.[1]

He echoes the thinking behind Henry Ford's popular statement, "Whether you think you can or think you can't, you're right." Lou goes on to say, "Whatever you repeatedly tell yourself with your own self-talk determines your beliefs and self-image, which affect your behavior." When Lou facilitated his workshops at Caterpillar, he gave us insight into our own self-talk through a homework assignment. He asked us to monitor our self-talk for a 24-hour period and see how much of the dialog was negative and how much was positive.

To further prove the point, he asked us to wear a rubber band around our wrist and snap it each time we caught ourselves having a negative thought about ourselves or someone else. Through that little exercise I quickly learned just how many of my thoughts were negative and learned how to stop the negative flow by saying to myself "Stop it. I'm better than that. Next time I'll ..." and finish the statement with a positive thought or action.

As I mentor young employees and work with those who lead them, I find that shaping self-talk is a critical piece of the puzzle when it comes to people believing they have the ability to execute a plan or achieve a goal. Whether they struggle with speaking in front of groups, traveling to unfamiliar places or meeting new people, helping them discover the basis for their fear and then adjusting their self-talk to address that fear is a good first step.

I often start the dialog by asking, "What are you afraid of?" If they hesitate, I encourage them by saying, "Ask yourself. You know." An employee who avoids public speaking may say he or she is afraid of "freezing" or forgetting their words. Someone who avoids networking may say they are afraid of reaching out to someone they don't know to make an introduction because they don't know what to say to start the conversation and then don't know what to say next. If someone avoids travel, it may be because they're afraid they'll get lost in unfamiliar surroundings.

Perfect! Once we have insight into the basis of the fear, we have something to work with. When an employee names the fear we can address it, put an action plan in place to overcome it and ultimately eliminate it. This is another place where you can differentiate yourself as a leader with this generation. They want to learn from you and if you can share your experience of overcoming a fear and moving forward to grow or change, your experience and success may be the impetus they need to do the same. In addition, your transparency and vulnerability also build trust and support a "fess it and fix it" culture.

As an example, let's take the employee who is afraid of public speaking, since that is a common fear. In fact, experts estimate that more than 75% of the population has some anxiety about public speaking so this is a fear that extends beyond cultures and generations.

In her book, *Speak*, Sally Lou Oaks Loveman addresses the fear of public speaking and puts it into perspective when she says, "People fear public speaking over death, heights and bugs." She adds humor by recounting a Jerry Seinfeld joke that "people would rather be in the coffin than deliver the eulogy." She goes on to say that "speaking is like everything we do. It's a practice."[2]

Given that thought, how can you help an employee practice externally and internally? External practice might include:

- Physically or virtually visiting the place where they'll be speaking so they can get comfortable with the stage or surroundings.
- Writing out the main message points—not a script, but the main topics—and working with them to "dry run" or practice several times a day until they develop "muscle memory" and can give the presentation or recall the talking points with limited notes or none at all.
- Working with them on the cadence of their words, points of emphasis and tone of voice until the delivery feels natural.

When an employee sees progress through the external practice, they may begin to believe they can be successful and be ready to add internal practice with self-talk. Internal practice might include:

- Asking them to visualize a time in the past when they were successful, vividly recall how that felt and then describe what they were feeling, physically and emotionally.
- Inviting them to transition the past success to the upcoming presentation and imagine themselves being equally successful this time.
- Encouraging them to practice looking forward positively by seeing their success as if it already happened and then writing an affirmation or summary statement to affirm it—as if it were true right now.
- Asking them to repeat the affirmation over and over in their mind, each time feeling the positive emotions attached to their success.
- Reminding them that the more they keep this visual top of mind, the sooner they will begin to behave like the new picture they've envisioned.

Through these tactics you've not only helped an employee overcome a fear of public speaking but more importantly you've given them a process to overcome future fears, enabling them to take on challenges that they feel are too big for them—ones that will ultimately allow them to move beyond their comfort zone and grow. Win-win!

Expanding positive self-talk to positive team-talk

If you want to take this concept of positive thinking beyond the individual and extend it to your entire team to create a culture of positivity, here are a couple of ideas:

- Begin each staff meeting with "Celebrations," recognizing things the team members have learned or accomplished since the last meeting. Take a minute to "revel" with them and watch the tone of the meeting become more positive from the outset.
- Encourage your team to share "Good Gossip" with one another between staff meetings. Good gossip works the same way as bad gossip, so we all know how to do it. In its simplest form, ask your employees to find out something positive about someone on the team and tell three people. That's it. Quick. Simple. Positive.
- Introduce the "Tell me something good" game. It's easy to play and uplifting. Each team member commits to having a positive thought, saying or humorous story in mind at all times. Whenever another team

member needs a boost, he or she can reach out to a peer with the request "tell me something good," and the team member responds with their positive thought or story, no questions asked. This gives employees a safe way to ask for encouragement when they need it without any further explanation about what might be troubling them.

- End each staff meeting with the question, "What are you looking forward to?" This ends the meeting on a high note and gets the team focusing forward—positively.

Another area of interest for today's employees is personal productivity. They're curious about how you get your work done without stressing, what tools you use to stay organized and suggestions you can share with them for either one. Let's take a look at ways to do that in the next segment.

IDENTIFY PERSONAL PRODUCTIVITY TOOLS YOU'VE FOUND SUCCESSFUL

Today's employees have apps. Loads of them. They can schedule meetings, download project plans, update To Do lists and chat with multiple team members around the globe, all at the same time. And when they feel themselves getting stressed, they can go to their meditation app and do some instructor- led deep breathing. Technology is not the issue here. Most any hurdle they face will involve understanding people and processes, and those insights come from experience. They're looking for your expertise in managing these and adapting to varying workloads with multiple deadlines.

Millennials are eager to prove their value by contributing good work and innovative ideas, both of which they hope will position them to advance. As a result, they may say "yes" to multiple tasks they're not equipped to handle or volunteer to take on additional assignments when they don't fully understand the workload they already have or how best to accomplish it. This is where you can help.

An employee's need may be as simple as prioritizing their workload. Here are some questions you can ask them to get them going in the right direction:

- Do you have one complete list of all of your tasks and the corresponding deadlines so you understand your entire workload?
- Which tasks are urgent and which are important?
- Can you break down each main goal or task into subtasks?

- Are some subtasks contingent on others? If so, can you arrange them in the order they need to happen?
- How much time do you estimate each task and subtask will take?
- Which tasks can you complete yourself, and which ones require collaboration?
- What three things do you have to get done today?

Once they have answered these questions, ask them to block time on their calendars to do specific work and only that work. They may find the very time they spend worrying about getting the work done is a distraction in itself and a waste of time—time they could be using to complete the task. If they are easily distracted, "Focus & Finish" is a mantra I learned that helps keep me on track with a singular task until it is completed. If they are deadline driven, estimating the time required to complete a task and then setting an alarm for that amount of time may also be helpful. We tend to use whatever time we have available so setting a limited time may spur on productivity.

If you have an employee who always seems really busy but isn't getting work done, having a conversation with them about the difference between being busy and productive may be a good next step. Dr. Thomas Roedl, also known as "Tom Solid," founded the "Paperless Movement" and wrote an article entitled, "Effectiveness and Efficiency—the Secret Ingredients of Productivity." In it he explains,

- Effectiveness is comparing what you <u>can get</u> done (your capacity) with what you actually got done (your results).
- Efficiency is doing more with less. It's the measure of how well you perform a task with the least waste of resources like time, money, energy, and materials.

Productivity depends on the quality of your production process or personal workflow to get things done.[3] In a recent *Forbes* article, entitled "Busy vs. Productive: Which One Are You?" Jennifer Cohen describes being productive as "moving the ball a few inches closer to the goal every single day." She further breaks down that notion into four simple steps:

- Focus on one thing at a time, identifying which one thing will deliver the most results first.
- "Chunk" your time each day based on goals and tasks you need to get done first.
- Think smaller. Break the long-term goals down into smaller weekly or daily goals.

- Master your calendar. Log your activity for a few days, and determine where time is productive and wasted.[4]

While it's true that no one has total control of their calendar or the tasks that might crop up on a given day, helping employees pay attention to what they can control often produces a leap in productivity. Cohen concurs with this thinking when she writes, "The most productive and efficient people are those who 'own their day' versus letting their day own them. They work to maximize their time to be as productive as possible."

The tool I use and share the most for helping employees construct their workflow to be "their most productive" is one I learned at Purina. It's called "**Timing & Thresholds,**" and you can find it in the "Leadership Tools" section in the back of this book.

This tool helps employees understand which tasks energize and drain them, what people energize and drain them, how many tasks of a certain type they can manage well in a given day, and what timing is best for each task. Given this information that is unique to the individual, they can structure their "custom-made" day to be more efficient and productive. They may also find that tracking the number of hours they work every week, including phone time, texting or checking email from home, may give them insight into their productivity rhythm and "sweet spot," where they produce the most work in the least amount of time.

What if an employee does the work to define their most productive day and then looks ahead to see a day that is overloaded, knowing it's one they can't change? Remind them of the things they can control—like monitoring their positive self-talk or taking a few extra minutes to revitalize throughout a back-to-back day. You can also ask them what they're looking forward to, encouraging them to focus forward, positively, beyond the next few hours.

What if they have a day that goes completely upside down? What if something or someone presents a situation or engages in a conversation that they didn't see coming or weren't prepared to handle in the moment? These are the things that can set an employee's mind in a downward spiral of negative self-talk called "reeling," which can quickly impact productivity, sometimes for days. Someone who is "reeling" is often so fixated on an incident or conversation that they can't think of anything else and they spend time "sharing" the incident with coworkers, which further impacts productivity. So how can you help them stop the "reeling?"

"**Separating Issues from Emotions**" is another tool I learned at Purina, and it's designed to stop the "reeling." It's also consistently rated as a "most valuable," tool by my workshop attendees. You'll find it in the Tools section in the back of this book. In its simplest form, this tool impacts efficiency and productivity by helping employees summarize a stressful situation or conversation, identify the emotions they feel as a result and articulate the things they can impact, which becomes their action plan. With a little practice, employees soon find they can do this exercise in their head and quickly move from emotional "reeling" to identifying issues they can impact and a plan they can execute. Ultimately, they spend less time "reeling" and more time being productive.

Sometimes employees find there is a certain person or recurring meeting that is a consistent source of irritation or frequently ends in "reeling." If you've experienced this on your team, another tool to share with employees is **Tracking Behavior Patterns to Bring Out the Best in All of Us.** You'll find this one in the Leadership Tools section at the back of this book as well.

The premise here is simple. People are very consistent, and they often repeat the same behavior or series of behaviors in the same order. If we can teach our employees to pay attention to the sequencing of another person's behavior, they may see a pattern. If they see a pattern of behavior, they may be able to get ahead of it and possibly change the person's behavior by the way they pro-act or react.

Here's an example. One of the women I mentor was struggling with a project manager who was a peer on her team. She felt like each meeting with that person was an interrogation about the status of her projects. She had included her updates in the project plan, so she thought that information had been communicated and she was ready to move on to next steps. They could never seem to get on the same page or make progress. Each meeting felt exactly like the previous one, and both team members were frustrated.

I shared this tool with her and instead of being annoyed by his questions, she wrote them down. Instead of internalizing his negative comments she challenged herself to translate them by asking "What does he need?" and "How can I help him?" Through her analysis each week she learned he was asking questions regarding the "why" behind the work. He really wanted to know how she had arrived at some of the decisions and what factors were considered in the decision making. He wanted to better understand her whole process and be able to explain it to others.

Once she understood his need and why it was important to him, she took time during the meetings to review the project status, identify the decision points and summarize the alternatives considered. As her style changed, so did his. He had fewer and fewer questions. The tone of the meeting became more collaborative, and they began to work together to move the project forward.

You probably have had similar experiences and may have coached your employees through some as well. Each one of these productivity tools is really a process that helps them get to the root cause of the issue they're dealing with. And the faster we can help them get to the root cause, the faster they'll be able to address it and improve it.

DIRECT ME TO SELF-MANAGEMENT, PERSONAL PRODUCTIVITY RESOURCES

Depending on the size of your company, you may have an HR resource or intranet learning site with self-management and personal productivity resources. There may also be an internal social media network where employees can ask each other to recommend or evaluate resources they've used. Given the work/life integration of today's employees, audio books and podcasts that they can listen to in small segments, or during a commute, seem to be preferred. Following are a few websites, blogs and articles that you could share with your employees as an extension of your conversations about self-management and personal productivity:

> https://www.lifehack.org/
>
> https://thepacificinstitute.com/
>
> https://www.businessballs.com/
>
> https://hbr.org/topic/managing-yourself
>
> https://www.huffpost.com/entry/leading-by-example-a-guid_b_7270048
>
> http://www.careerizma.com/blog/self-management-skills/
>
> https://www.headspace.com/

In addition to understanding your self-care tips and personal productivity tools, today's employees want to learn about your leadership style. That's what we'll delve into next in Chapter 8. They want to know how you articulate your style, where you learned it and why it's important to you.

As future leaders, your employees are information gatherers: listening to what you say and watching how you lead, using both to determine their own leadership style. One of my mentees recently told me, "I feel like I have catapulted my career by 10 years just by learning from your mistakes. Now I won't make those mistakes, although I'm sure I'll make plenty of my own." Don't we all!

CHAPTER 8

LEADERSHIP STYLES THAT WORK FOR YOU

THERE IS NO END TO THE leadership resources available to millennials. There are audio books, podcasts, webinars and virtual workshops—all providing insight on how to be an effective leader. What today's employees really want to know is what is YOUR leadership style, how did you develop it, and why is it important to you. From their perspective, you are a significant benchmark, and your definition and lessons learned will help them mold their own style.

In this chapter, we'll look at three ways you can share your knowledge and leave a legacy. Here's what today's employees value most from you:

- Understand and articulate your leadership style.
- Share your lessons learned.
- Identify leadership skills you've seen demonstrated & ones to develop.
- Recommend leadership development resources, role models and opportunities.

Now let's look at each one of these in more detail. Think back to when you were formulating a leadership style or recognized one you wanted to adopt. That's likely where many of your young employees are today, and it's a place where you can add lasting value.

UNDERSTAND AND ARTICULATE YOUR LEADERSHIP STYLE

Your leadership style is likely a composite of pieces you learned from lots of different leaders and people who were important in your life, as well as lessons you've learned the hard way. There are multiple academic leadership styles, ranging from directive to transactional and collaborative to transformational.

Most style guides also encourage leaders to be practiced in several styles as part of their toolbox so they can accommodate a variety of leadership situations. Whatever your style, name it and be able to articulate the reason behind it. Why is that important?

William "Bill" Taylor, cofounder of *Fast Company* and author of *Simply Brilliant: How Great Organizations Do Ordinary Things in Extraordinary Ways*, asks and answers that question for us: "Why is it important to gain clarity about the leadership style that fits each of us best? Because the more we understand about ourselves — what we truly care about, how we make decisions, why we do what we do — the more effective we will be at marshaling the support of others for what we hope to achieve." [1]

The most significant part of marshaling the support of others to achieve goals is understanding the "why" behind your leadership style and being able to communicate it to others in a meaningful way. Let's look at an example.

Know Your WHY

Whether your decision to become a leader was the result of a pivotal moment in your career or a culmination of a series of events, at some point you knew you wanted to lead. When you think about sharing this with an employee, how would you summarize that event or sequence of events and the impact it had on you? In other words, "What's your WHY?" This is what employees want to know and they want the authentic version, not the edited one. Here's mine.

As I shared in Chapter 3, when I told my boss, Neal, that my husband had been transferred and I was leaving Purina, he orchestrated a six-month learning plan that would enable me to become the leader he envisioned me to be, albeit at another company. That was the first part of the story. Here's the rest.

For six months, my husband traveled to his new job through the week and was home on weekends. Our jobs were going well, we were making the long-distance marriage work, and our two- and four-year old boys seemed to be adjusting. Our house hadn't sold, we loved our babysitter, and I was getting accustomed to the role of single, married mom. I told Neal that our new family dynamic was working just fine, and I had decided not to make the move. Since we hadn't made the formal announcement, I thought he would be pleased, and life as we knew it would continue.

Boy, was I wrong! When I shared my new plan with Neal, his response was emphatic, "We're done here. I've taught you what you need to know. It's time for us to let you go. And it's time for you to let us go. We're not splitting a family over a job—not on my watch. You have six weeks to find a new job, plan your move, and get your family back together. Then we'll make the announcement to our employees and customers that you're leaving. Our next goal is an exit strategy. Let's get moving."

With that, he applied the same gusto and urgency to creating my exit plan as he had my learning plan. He hired a headhunter to identify potential companies and roles that would be a good fit for me, he reviewed my resume, and he helped me with interview prep. Sure enough, in six weeks I had an offer, and we were ready to announce my departure. As the employee meeting approached where Neal was going to make the announcement, he gave me one last assignment—one I'll always remember.

He said, "Beginning tomorrow and for the rest of your life people will ask you why you left Purina. Your assignment is to create a scripted statement that will be your response to that question for years to come. The statement needs to explain why you're leaving, but more importantly why it's positive for you—not for your husband or your family or anyone else—why it's positive for you. Do you know why this is important? Because this is the type of situation that can cause a wedge in your marriage for the rest of your life, and we're not going to let that happen."

I didn't sleep much that night as I was wrestling with my assignment, but by morning I was ready. When asked why I was leaving Purina, I responded, "My husband has been made a partner in his firm, which is his dream, but if it hadn't been for his company we wouldn't have moved to St. Louis and I wouldn't have had the opportunity to work for Purina, a company that changed my life."

Through tears of gratitude, I thanked Neal for my final assignment and all that he had invested in me and asked, "How can I ever repay this company that has given so much to me?" He responded, "Kathryn, you repay Purina every time you take what you've learned and help someone else." I vowed that day that I would do whatever I could each and every day to repay Purina, by taking what I learned and helping someone else. Why do I lead and teach and mentor? That's my WHY.

What's the take-away here? The leadership style I experienced and adopted is servant leadership—that is leading by serving others. This means making others' needs a priority, seeing the best in them and helping them see the best in themselves. I know in any given situation if I'm asking the questions, "What do they need?" and "How can I help them?" I'm on the right path.

Abby Wambach, U.S. Soccer Olympic Gold Medalist and author of the book, "Wolfpack" defines servant leadership this way. "Leader is not a title that the world gives you—it's an offering that you give the world."[2] I like her definition too. Whatever your style, name it, claim it and share your WHY.

When I share these stories with those I lead and mentor or those who join me for a workshop, I ask them what they are thinking and feeling. The responses range from tears to silence to a proclamation like, "That's the kind of leader I want to be," which was my reaction when I experienced this style of leadership too. Another response I frequently hear is "That's the kind of leader I wish I had." My response to them is a challenge in the words of Mahatma Gandhi, who said "Be the change you want to see in the world." In short, the next generation of great leaders can begin with you.

SHARE YOUR LESSONS LEARNED

Once you've identified your leadership style and defined your "why," think about your lessons learned—the good, the bad and the ugly. Sharing these is another opportunity to build trust through transparency and contribute to the development of an aspiring leader. Don't be afraid to share your "Lousy Leader" stories and more importantly, share the lessons you learned from them and how you incorporate those learnings into your leadership style today.

One of the "Lousy Leader" moments that I often share began with me complaining to my boss about a co-worker. I recounted all the mistakes my peer was making in operations and with his team, and then I explained the impact it was having on customers. Of course, he would take my side, right? My boss' response was not what I expected. He asked, "Have you talked to him about these things?" Of course, I had not, which I reluctantly admitted.

At that point, my boss gave me an assignment to go talk to my peer, work out our differences, put a plan together to solve the problems and be in his office at 8am the next morning to share the plan with him. Together. Yikes! This was not going the way I had envisioned. Now I had to go to my peer and tell him I was "tattling" on him to our boss. On top of that, we were going to have to take time that afternoon to resolve our differences and develop a plan that we could share with our boss the next morning. Needless to say, my peer was furious, and rightfully so. We agreed to meet later that afternoon, sort through our differences and create a plan.

The next morning when we met with our boss, he listened to our plan and then turned to me and said, "There were three meetings here Kathryn. One with you and me. One with the two of you, and one with all three of us. Two of those meetings were unnecessary. The next time you have a problem with a peer, go talk to your peer, not to me. The only meeting that was necessary was the one you two had yesterday to work out your differences and put a plan in place to make any changes. The other two meetings were a waste of time. Don't do it again."

I certainly learned this lesson the hard way, and I never did it again. Because I knew how impactful it was to bring both parties together, I also practiced this tactic as a leader when I had one team member complain about another. I found that bringing both parties together resolved the issue quickly and ultimately eliminated the behavior. This is also a great way to reduce the amount of negative employee meetings you have to manage.

Another way to reduce the negativity is to set a time limit. As leaders, we are sometimes given a directive to execute that doesn't make sense to us. We know when this happens that our boss may have more information that can't be shared right then or our boss may be just "executing" a higher level directive as well. I've found in these situations it's best to "challenge and champion" the directive with my boss and model that leadership for my employees. Here's how.

I would bring my team together, explain the directive and set a timer for five minutes, explaining that we had five minutes to express our "challenges" as a team. When the timer sounded, we were done "challenging" and would agree to focus our energy and conversation toward ways to "champion" the request. How do you motivate a team to tackle something that doesn't make sense to you or to them? Set Logic Aside. Yep! Sometimes the quickest way to move forward is not to argue the merit of the assignment but rather Set Logic Aside and focus on how to execute well and quickly, together.

Sharing the genesis of your lessons learned and the logic behind why you choose to lead the way you do can open an ongoing dialog with employees. Ask for their feedback too. Are there components of your leadership style that really resonate with them? Are there ones they'd like to learn more about? This dialog leads us to our next area of discovery and disclosure.

IDENTIFY LEADERSHIP SKILLS YOU'VE SEEN DEMONSTRATED & ONES TO DEVELOP

As employees are gathering leadership information and formulating their own style, they're looking to you as a sounding board. They want to know if they're on track in terms of leadership development. As you see them demonstrate good leadership skills, recognize the behavior you want them to repeat and give them specific examples of what you've seen them do well.

By the same token, as you see them demonstrating "Lousy Leader" or self-serving tendencies, have a candid conversation with them about that too. Tell them what you've seen, give specific examples and offer a course correction as quickly as possible. Much like the self-talk dialog we discussed in Chapter 7 your talking points with an aspiring leader can be, "I know you can do better

than that. Next time I'd like to see you _____" and fill in the blank with
the desired behavior. Direct. Specific. Actionable.

One of the hardest transitions for first-time supervisors to make is migrat-
ing from a peer to a boss. Learning how to build relationships and demonstrate
genuine concern for employees and still be able to have a tough conversation
with them is part of a learning curve as a leader. Developing the ability to accept
constructive input or even harsh words from employees and translate them
into something actionable is part of a growth path as well. Here's an example.

Forgiveness is Part of Leadership

You've heard lots of Neal Lewis stories from me already, but here's another
lesson that was really impactful and stayed with me throughout my career. As a
new supervisor, I'd just been through my first round of employee opinion sur-
veys where employees gave candid, anonymous feedback about their boss. My
results were not good. In fact, some of the employee comments about me were
downright hurtful—or so I thought. I wasn't mature enough as a leader to look
past the harsh words or be able to translate them into some constructive action
I could take. Instead, I sat in my office with the door closed and pouted.

Neal gave me a day to cool down but the next day he came in for a chat. Instead of chastising me for the way I was acting he took a few minutes to look at
the cards I had on my desk, knowing they were things that revitalized me. One
of the cards was from an employee, and it had some very kind words about my
leadership and the impact I had on that person. Neal handed me the card and
asked me to read it. I said he could read it. He handed it to me again and said,
"I'm asking you to read it. Out loud. To me."

This time I complied, reluctantly. When I finished reading the card he asked,
"Is that the leader you are today? The one described in this card?" I had to admit
I was not, but in my defense, I said I was mad and hurt by the things that were
said in the employee opinion survey. Neal acknowledged my feelings and said,
"You know as leaders, our job is to give first and give again. Do you know what
the bridge is between giving first and giving again?" When I shook my head,
he said "For." When I admitted I wasn't following his logic, he said, "Forgive."

I said, "Oh, forgiveness." He said, "No. Forgiveness is a noun. That's something someone else does. Forgive is a verb, and that's what I want to see you do.
Forgive." He went on to explain, "Forgiveness is an important part of leadership. I want to see you master this because if you don't this is something that
will hold you back for the rest of your career. There will be times when you have
to forgive your employees, your peers and your leaders in order for you to move
on and be the leader you were meant to be."

Neal retired a few years after I left Purina, and he went on to do full-time ministry work. When he passed away, I felt like the world stopped for a moment and gave thanks for a life well lived and a man well loved. I will be forever grateful for the difference he made in my life and the investment he made in me as a leader. As I pass along his stories and my lessons learned I still feel him with me and know he is helping others through me. Not long after I retired from Caterpillar, one of the women I mentored posted a message on social media recounting a leadership lesson she had learned and closed by saying, "and the legacy of Neal Lewis lives on." Perfect.

The conversation Neal had with me about forgiveness was the genesis for the "Hero Page" tool that is in the Leadership Tools section in the back of the book. It's one you can use yourself (Be Your Own Hero) and share with your employees. It provides a place to record positive things you've learned about a person, things they've accomplished and reasons why you respect and admire them— whether they're a leader, a peer or a team member. Why is that important? Three reasons.

First, recording positive things you've learned about someone else is uplifting to you, and if you let them know you've made an entry on their Hero page and why, it can be uplifting to them too. I would often send an email with a subject line of "You're My Hero." The message might be as simple as, "Heroes are people who act with courage and you just did. Thank you for your courageous leadership."

Second, at some point you're going to have a tough day with that person. When you do, turning to their Hero Page reminds you of all the things you respect and admire about them and puts the day's events in perspective.

Third, at some point, your Hero is going to have a tough day and what an encouragement you will be to them when you remind them of the things you've watched them accomplish and affirm that the person who did those things could surely handle whatever's in front of them today.

Another important leadership skill to look for in aspiring leaders is perseverance. As cliché as it sounds, sometimes the path to growth is made up of a million baby steps—mostly forward. This leadership lesson is one I learned before I ever entered the corporate world, and it came from an unlikely source— my flight instructor.

Perseverance: Progress Over Perfection

Early in my career, I worked for a helicopter magazine called "Rotor & Wing International." I was a young editor right out of journalism school, and I soon learned that the publisher wanted all the editors for this magazine to go to flight school so we could understand our subject matter and better converse with the pilots who were our contributing editors. My flight instructor was the Chief Pilot at a small regional airport, and he told me that he would be teaching me how to fly and passing on some life lessons along the way.

One bright, sunny Saturday morning when I showed up at the airport, my instructor let me know that my lesson that day would be to land in a cornfield. When I asked him why he said, "Because I want you to know that you can." I knew instinctively this was going to be a "life lesson" as well as a "flight lesson" day. Sure enough, after I'd done my share of "touch and go" exercises, which is a series of landings and immediate take offs, he had me reach altitude and then picked out a cornfield where he instructed me to land, just like we'd been doing all morning—minus the runway. As I touched down in the cornfield, the landing was a lot bumpier than usual but to my surprise, it was still controlled. When I brought the aircraft to a complete stop, my instructor asked, "You alive?" I responded, "Yes." He continued, "You're alive. I'm alive. Good landing."

As we taxied across the cornfield over to the airport, I asked him which part of the training that day was my life lesson: landing in a corn field or living through it? He said, "Both. As a pilot and in life, it's important to know you can land in unlikely surroundings and come out of it stronger and more confident than you started. It's also good to know that some days the measure of success is simply living through it. On those days, ask yourself, 'You alive?' Answer yourself, 'I'm alive.' And then remind yourself, 'Good landing.'"

This is sometimes a hard lesson for young employees to learn. Some want to do things perfectly and may even pride themselves on being perfectionists. That can be dangerous for an aspiring leader because there's little about leadership that goes perfectly as planned. In fact, much of leadership requires the ability to be flexible and "pivot" while still making progress. As you see your young employees demonstrating this skill, take a moment to recognize it as a valuable leadership trait that will serve them well.

The second leadership lesson I learned in flight school takes the idea of pivoting one step further. When I was learning to fly, one of the toughest skills for me to master was a maneuver called "stalls and spins." Not only was it required to pass the course, it was vital knowledge for any pilot to have in case an engine failed. I was flying single-engine planes which made this skill even more critical. The exercise basically taught you how to recover the aircraft to a level state if the engine failed and then prepared you for landing if necessary. Here's how it worked.

You began by taking the aircraft up to a fairly high altitude and then pulling the stick (which looks like a wheel) back towards you until the nose of the airplane was straight up and the aircraft was perpendicular to the ground. Now the plane doesn't want to do this anymore than you do, so it takes some upper body strength and sheer determination to hold the aircraft in this position at full speed. In a matter of minutes, the engine would stall and the most awful foghorn sound would alert the pilot that the engine had failed.

At the same time, the aircraft would nosedive and spin in a downward spiral. FAST. As a pilot, all you could see was the ground coming up toward you as you continued to spin in circles. Not only was this disorienting, but if you're prone to any type of vertigo or motion sickness, the speed and spiral are not a good combination.

At this point in the exercise, every instinct within your very being tells you to pull back on the stick and lean back in the seat to avert the ground coming up at you. Although it's not intuitive, the only way to level the plane is to push forward. When you push through the spin toward the very ground you are trying to avoid, the engine gets air and recovers from the stall. The plane miraculously returns to level flying and once again... you're in control...and ready to climb.

The first time I did this maneuver successfully, my instructor cheered and said, "You and I have slain a dragon today. It won't be the last one you face but this same process will serve you well. When you hit a stall in life, push through the spin, toward the very thing that scares you and that simple act will bring you back to straight and level...and you'll be ready to climb."

What's the take-away here? Perseverance is pushing through the sirens, and the stalls, and the spins. Sometimes your young employees can run on sheer willpower and push through whatever is in front of them without stopping. Other times they may need to stop, regroup, and start again. And they need to know that's ok.

I learned this lesson of stopping and starting again when I was in chemotherapy treatment for breast cancer. Since my cancer was very aggressive, my treatment needed to be too, so I often spent a few days in the hospital following treatment. After one particularly tough round, I turned to my husband, Scott and said, "I think this thing could really get me. What are we going to do?"

Without missing a beat, he said, "We're going to get through the next 10 minutes, and then the next. And pretty soon we'll get through an hour, and then the next. And then a day, and then the next. And before long, we'll be on the other side of this, right here together where we belong." That day we coined the term "10-Minute Days," and we had a few of them.

Your employees may have some 10-minute days too. They may stop and start and stop again before they gain some momentum. Whatever their speed or style, recognizing their tenacity and their progress over perfection is something that will help them develop a solid foundation for leadership and for life.

RECOMMEND LEADERSHIP DEVELOPMENT RESOURCES, ROLE MODELS AND OPPORTUNITIES

Another way you can help young leaders grow and develop is by introducing them to leaders in other areas of the company or connecting them with leaders who have roles similar to yours in other companies within your industry. Setting up informational interviews or job shadowing days for them can also offer insight into various leadership roles and styles.

You can help them get the most out of these experiences by asking them to come prepared with a list of questions to ask and topics to discuss. Some companies also offer "exchange" programs for employees of companies within a member organization or industry group, and this might be another way to broaden an employee's exposure to leadership.

Other resources might include a community leadership development program through the Chamber of Commerce or volunteer leadership opportunities through local charities or nonprofit organizations that are of interest to them. You can also challenge your employees to do their own research and come back to you with a list of leadership development opportunities that interest them and then create a plan together. This can be a very powerful activity and a rare opportunity to influence your employees in a significant way.

To this point we talked about identifying your employee's strengths and transferable skills. We've reviewed self-care and personal productivity tools and discussed leadership styles and lessons learned. As we move into Chapter 9, we'll see how all of these pieces work together to help employees utilize their creativity and innovation to create a vision, and articulate it in a way that inspires and engages others to take an idea from concept to execution.

CHAPTER 9

CREATIVITY AND INNOVATION STRATEGIES

THIS IS THE CHAPTER where everything you've read so far comes together. You'll see how all the pieces build on one another and how your employees' development will evolve. This evolution ultimately benefits you because as your employees become more self-sufficient and independent, you'll become less and less involved in their day-to-day tasks and team management—which gives you even more opportunity to focus on leadership—your true gift.

Let's review our journey together so far. We began in Chapters 1 and 2 focusing on the fundamental things that millennials want from their boss like clear expectations, ongoing honest feedback, and developmental assignments. Setting clear goals with defined measurements and rewards are the first step. Holding them accountable to meet those goals and being consistent with your leadership style are the next steps in building a solid foundation of trust. These four steps from Chapter 2 are key:

- Review a job description (beyond the job posting) with specifics about the responsibilities.
- Provide consistent training, standard work or processes for the basic tasks required.
- Set three to five goals with a measurable outcome, timeline, and definition of success.
- Explain the compensation or reward structure.

Creating regular employee "touchpoints" like we reviewed in Chapter 2 will also help you continue the dialog and establish more trust milestones. One of those "touchpoints" is regular one-on-one meetings, using the **"3-Bucket Exercise"** format outlined in Chapter 2. It looked like this:

BUCKET 1: "Ah-Ha" (things I learned, completed, want to celebrate)

BUCKET 2: "Hmmmm" (things I'm aware of, want to learn more about, need an action plan for)

BUCKET 3: "What in the world?" (things I don't understand, didn't realize were part of the job or life in general or seem overwhelming)

In Chapter 3, we learned that using one-on-one meetings to get to know your employees personally is important to them. This includes learning about their families, their hobbies, and the person they want to become, as well as understanding what motivates them to succeed, what revitalizes them and what genuine recognition looks like for them. The "Getting to Know You" questions from Chapter 3 include each of these topics plus information on how to apply the feedback in a way that fosters transparency.

In Chapters 4 and 5, we discovered how employees want someone to share their potential, help them navigate their careers and sponsor them for advancement. These ongoing "connection builders" are key to their engagement and ultimately their loyalty, as are flexible schedules and the ability to work remotely.

Chapter 6 explained that employees are looking for a strong sense of purpose from you as their leader and also from their company. It's important for them to know the work they do matters and serves a greater purpose. To them, these conversations are more relationship builders and trust milestones that further cement their engagement.

Chapters 7 and 8 provided insight into how to help them develop a leadership style, manage their own self-care and increase personal productivity. This is where the tide starts to turn, and the firm foundation you've laid begins to pay off. The faster you lay a solid foundation in terms of your relationship with your employees, the faster you get to this point of return on your investment – leadership development for them and their loyalty for you.

Here's the practical application. Remember the leadership tools we identified in Chapter 8 to support employees in managing their own self-care, interacting well with others and increasing productivity? As employees raise issues during your one-on-one meetings, empower them to problem solve using these tools *as they need them*. Why? Three reasons:

1. Introducing the tools all at once can be overwhelming and less effective.

2. Utilizing their creativity and innovation is important for them and for you.

3. Problem-solving is a skill you want them to master as part of their leadership development.

When you share one tool at a time, you can choose the tool that would benefit that employee the most at that point in time. Meet them where they are. That's also the time and place where they are most open to learning because they see the potential for an immediate personal benefit. They understand that the time to apply that tool is now and can recognize when to use it again in the future. The order in which you introduce the tools may be different for each employee, depending on their current need, and that's ok.

How do you know what would help them and when? This is where the "3-bucket" discussion format provides the perfect conversation starter. Anything an employee identifies in Bucket 2 or Bucket 3 requires problem solving, and keep in mind, the problem they want to solve may be personal or professional (Remember, mine was trying to get dinner on the table!).

Problem Solving for Leadership Development

You can help employees take some initial steps in their own problem solving by asking them to ask themselves these questions before they come to you:

1. Have you seen anything like this before? If so, what worked well to resolve it?

2. Who else do you know who may have solved a similar problem? What did they do?

3. If someone brought this issue to you, what would you tell them to do or what questions would you have for them?

Some of my best leaders and mentors were so practiced at empowering me to self-discover through questions that it sometimes took months or even years for me to realize they had the answer all along but they were using a line of questions to help me get to the solution on my own. Not only did this build my confidence, the questions they asked gave me a repeatable template for problem solving. They also reinforced the behavior by recognizing my "good idea" or "great problem solving" when in fact they had asked me a series of leading questions until I arrived at the solution "myself." You can do the same for your millennial team member, providing another gift from a "Good Leader."

If you think about the problems employees often bring to you that go beyond technical or skills-based training, they can usually be grouped into a handful of categories, each of which can be addressed with a Leadership Tool provided in the back of the book. With these, they can start "self-solving" recurring problems. Let's see how they match up.

PROBLEM	PROBLEM SOLVING LEADERSHIP TOOLS
Change, stress, anxiety, frustration	• Separating Issues from Emotions • What I Miss & What I Would Have Missed • Creating Your Vision—What Does Success Look Like? • Charting Your Path with a FROM/TO Exercise • Align Your Employees' Energy with Shared Goals
Self-care, balancing work and non-work life	• Mentor/Mentee Discussion Topics • 3 Things that Revitalize • Healthy Path
Interactions with co-workers, leaders, clients	• Hero Page • 3-Bucket Exercise • Good Gossip • Did it. Do it. Done. • Tracking Behavior Patterns to Bring Out the Best in All of Us
Managing multiple priorities, over commitment	• Set Them Up to Succeed—Clear Expectations • Start. Stop. Continue. • Cycle of Yes
Productivity, efficiency, time management, over analysis	• Timing & Thresholds • From Stuck to "Unstuck" • Focus & Finish
Confidence	• Top 10 List • Becoming the Person of Your Destiny • Positive Self-Talk & Affirmations
Having tough conversations Public speaking or presentations	• Just the Facts—Honest Evaluations • Talking Points for Tough Conversations • Role Play or Dry Run

You'll notice the first problem on this chart is change. Why? Because it's a constant. It's part of every role in every organization, all the time. It's part of life! Giving employees tools to manage change gives them control of an unknown and a positive path forward. It helps them define where they're going and why, which quickly leads to an action plan to get there. Here's an example.

Part of my role at the Caterpillar Visitors Center was managing the Corporate Archives. At the time it was a collection of papers, photos, and a few artifacts. As I learned more about our "collection," I realized these "things" had their own stories and more importantly they had people behind the stories that could bring our history to life, connecting the past to the present through exhibits at the Visitors Center. What a treasure!

Entrance into the archives was by appointment only. It was a beautiful space that was climate controlled and well organized. The contents could be retrieved by request and viewed on site by white-gloved attendees. This process worked well for preservation, not amplification. While I wanted to be respectful of the preservation process, I also wanted to share our stories with our world of customers, dealers, employees, and Cat fans. So how did we get from here to there? The From/To Chart.

It's really just a page with two columns: one labeled "From" and one labeled "To." Under the "From" heading we listed where we are today, and under the "To" heading we listed where we wanted to go. For the archives we wanted to move "From" a physical collection "To" a hybrid collection of physical and digital. We wanted to move "From" appointment only access "To" open visiting hours and scheduled tours. We wanted to move "From" artifacts being viewed on request "To" artifacts being shared publicly through exhibits and media. You get the idea.

Once we could identify the "From/To" transformation in five or six key areas we had our "picture" of success. Once we had that picture, we could summarize it into a statement, which became the vision we could articulate. Then we asked ourselves, "What three or four steps do we need to take to get 'From' where we are in each area 'To' where we want to go?" Those steps became our action plan. We asked ourselves how long it would take, what resources we would need and what the benefits would be. That became our business case—and we were off and running.

Do you see how this works? As leaders we give structure to the change, simplify the process and set the direction with the team. To gain their buy-in? Yes. To empower them? Yes. But mostly, they have good ideas. They're the experts in their craft, and our job is to channel their energy and knowledge toward the transformation that meets the business need. After they've done this once, they see how the process works and are more apt to use it again, especially if they're the ones who get to present their From/To idea and business case to leadership. Win, win!

As you share this tool and others with your employees, reinforce their success by reminding them of what has worked well for them before and asking them to recall the tool they used. Just like any other successful skill development, leadership is about applying a handful of simple tools well, consistently.

Remember Amber, one of our Rock Star Millennials? She is the one who was tasked with creating an internal call center as part of her marketing department. She had felt "stuck" for months trying to determine how to move forward. What was the key to getting her "unstuck?"

- Reviewing her past successes
- Creating a clear vision of what success looks like
- Breaking down the larger goal into smaller steps
- Defining tasks required to accomplish each step
- Assigning an owner, sequence and timeline for each task
- Incorporating positive self-talk, affirmations

As we talked through these steps during our weekly meetings, Amber saw her action items move from Bucket 3 to Bucket 2 to Bucket 1. Soon we were celebrating as much as planning! The process is simple and repeatable and provides a reference for future problem solving. Knowing the process and seeing the progress encouraged her to share more information and reach her goal more quickly.

After an employee has proven to themselves that the tool or process works, they will be much more likely to apply the same logic or tool to other aspects of their life and/or share it with others. When you give an employee a tool or outline a repeatable process that helps them solve their problem, it's a double win: they solved the problem and you earned a trust milestone. If it worked for them, it's also likely they will share it with others—an added bonus.

This is the beginning of the ripple effect and the way to scale these leadership tools throughout your organization. It's the power of one helping one.

Why is this important? When employees feel empowered, they're engaged. When they're engaged, they freely offer their creativity, innovation and discretionary effort. When this happens, they become our greatest resource. It's been said, "Our people are our greatest asset." I disagree. So did Neal Lewis. When he would hear someone say this, he would respond with a different thought. "People are NOT our greatest asset," he would say. "People are our greatest *resource*. Assets *depreciate* and people *appreciate* when they are nurtured and developed." I couldn't agree more!

When employees are nurtured and developed, they feel safe – and their energy and creativity kick into high gear. This is something you can only buy with earned trust and transparency. When employees turn this corner, they become unstoppable, and there seems to be no end to what they can accomplish, quickly.

If you've ever seen this transformation in an employee, you know what I'm talking about. If you, as a leader or a mentor, contributed to that metamorphosis, you feel like this is a pivotal moment where they see the light and you see their true potential. This is your return on investment. This is when your leadership comes full circle, and you take a step to the side as they step forward.

The Culmination of Leadership

When you've gotten an employee to this point and they're ready to charge ahead, where do they need your help next? Here's what they're asking for:

- Recognize my creativity & innovation.
- Help me develop proof of concept to take an idea from conception to execution.
- Teach me how to create a strategic business case for my ideas.

An employee's greatest challenge at this point is they don't know what they don't know. This is where your experience and expertise shines! Use your lessons learned to help them channel their newfound energy and translate their idea into a reality from a business standpoint – navigating the political landmines they may not be aware of along the way.

RECOGNIZE MY CREATIVITY & INNOVATION

Millennials are an entrepreneurial generation. They like inventing things. They're full of ideas. They pride themselves on being highly creative and innovative, often incorporating technology because it's a natural extension of ideas to them. Technology has been part of their life for as long as they can remember so using it to augment or illustrate an idea seems natural.

The best way to unleash this creativity and innovation is to recognize it and encourage it. This is where the relationship you've developed based on trust and transparency pays off, again.

Being innovative doesn't always mean creating something new. Sometimes it means improving something that already exists. At Purina, we often challenged ourselves to look at the work we were doing each day and ask, "How can we do this better, faster, or cheaper?" This is where innovation begins, and you can encourage it by asking your employees for their ideas. Trust me. They have them.

Another way to initiate this dialog is through an exercise called "Start. Stop. Continue." This is most effective in a team setting and is often productive when the group is going through a change in leadership, team dynamic, or strategic direction. Simply ask the team to think about the work they currently do and also think about the work they think they should be doing. Then ask each team member to identify which tasks the team should Start doing, Stop doing, and Continue doing.

Be sure to allow time for discussion too. Sometimes employees identify tasks to Stop doing because they don't understand the purpose of the task which gives you an opening to explain why it's important. You may also discover some employees are still doing tasks that you thought had been discontinued long ago or they've added tasks that are new to you and you may want to understand their value. Either way, the discussion is a viable one and may lead to some new ideas that benefit the business and empower the team.

I saw this firsthand at Caterpillar when I was working with the sustainability team. Each year, I was amazed at the great ideas that were generated as Caterpillar encouraged employee teams to submit their ideas for the annual Sustainability Awards. There was a formal submission process for capturing their innovations, and the submission included a problem statement and proposed solution or improvement, some of which originated with the simple "Start. Stop. Continue." discussion mentioned above.

The submission also included a plan to execute the idea and a summary of the investment required for assets and resources. Finally, the team identified the benefit to the business, the return on investment, timeline and/or the resulting benefit to the customer. I looked forward to reviewing these submissions every year as did our Sustainability Steering Committee and our External Sustainability Advisory Board. Together, we identified our top choices and forwarded them to the Executive Office to make the final selection.

The award winners were announced at the annual Leadership Summit, and teams of finalists were invited to attend an event that rivaled the Grammy Awards, or so we thought. Finalists for each category were announced before the winning team was revealed, and the award-winning team walked the "red carpet" to take their place on the stage and accept the award and accolades from the Chairman. The winning team received an engraved crystal award and had their photo taken with the Chairman. Their story was also shared internally with employees and externally through social media and the annual Sustainability Report.

This practice of inviting employee teams to submit their ideas and receive awards spurred even more creativity and innovation, which in turn led to more patents, new products, reduced costs and improved processes—a win/win for employees and the company.

HELP ME DEVELOP A PROOF OF CONCEPT TO TAKE AN IDEA FROM CONCEPT TO EXECUTION

Guiding your employees to develop a proof of concept is the next step in supporting their creativity and innovation. This is where they often get stuck and giving them a "proof of concept" assignment can help them move their idea from a thought to an action.

A proof of concept is nothing more than a small test case or sampling that proves the success of an idea on a small scale before investing the resources to institute a large-scale change. In marketing, this could be a trial offer to a certain customer segment. In production, it might be changing a portion of the assembly process before converting an entire line. In a cultural environment, it may be establishing flexible office hours for employees before moving to a hybrid or completely remote workforce.

In each instance, the test case or sampling provides "proof" that the idea has merit (or sometimes that it does not). Either way, there's some data or evidence to support the larger decision of whether or not to move forward to large-scale implementation that would require extensive time, attention, money and other resources. Sometimes the idea is valid but needs to be tweaked. Sometimes the timing just isn't right. Other times the idea may work in a controlled environment, but those controls also make it cost prohibitive to move forward. Here's an example.

When I worked at the Caterpillar Visitors Center, we had a young, enthusiastic and creative team. They had a new idea every minute! While I loved their enthusiasm, I also knew I needed to channel it, or our small staff would be overwhelmed with activity that might not be value added. As employees brought their ideas to the team, I learned quickly to ask for a proof of concept.

ADAM HAMILTON

ADAM HAMILTON, ANOTHER Rock Star Millennial who you'll learn more about shortly, was on my team and full of creative ideas. We opened the Visitors Center in October, and he joined us in December to work on marketing campaigns and exhibit events. Our team was always on the lookout for new revenue streams, and Adam had the idea of creating Christmas cards with im-

Adam Hamilton is the Director of Digital & Social for McDonald's

ages of antique tractors from our Corporate Archives. He brought the idea to me one afternoon, and I asked for a proof of concept. By that evening, he had created a dozen sets of four-pack Christmas cards, had packaged them nicely,and created a point-of-sale display for the ticketing desk in the lobby. We set them out the next morning, and by that weekend, we'd sold them all.

While we knew that creating and packaging these cards individually wouldn't be cost-effective in the long term, Adam proved on a small scale that there was an interest, and we ultimately worked with the Cat store and found a vendor to supply Caterpillar cards and postcards in a larger volume at a better price point for sale in the gift shop. We took Adam's good idea, tweaked it and made it even better.

In a few years Adam became a Caterpillar "alum," and he went on to McDonald's where he is currently the Director of Digital & Social. Before this role he was the Manager of Global Content & Editorial Planning, Manager of the Story Lab, and Supervisor of Leadership & Employee Communications.

How did Adam advance so quickly? He's innovative, collaborative and he raises his hand—a lot. In fact, he encourages other millennials to do the same. "You have to raise your hand and ask how you can help. That's how you get opportunities and get promoted," he said. "The reason I moved up so quickly is I kept getting on stretch projects. So many times, the leader is looking for someone with availability or someone who offers to help."

As Adam advanced in his career, he gained a different perspective. "As a leader, I see the other side. It's such a relief when someone is willing to help." He's also energized by his team. "They're engaged and creative and they feel like they work in a safe space. It's also good to get rid of all the politicking. Once that is gone, you can use all your energy in value-added work, which is what we want."

What were some of the challenges? "Showing an ROI. It's hard to do with communications. It's tough to find a true metric to tie to your work. That's why you have to be just as creative with KPIs (Key Performance Indicators) as you are with content. Whether you tie it to your food reputation or employee engagement, it has to be something you can measure."

When he thought about his lessons learned, Adam recalled two. "I still use the 90-Day Log (Buckets 1,2,3) I learned at Caterpillar to onboard new employees. It helps us be super transparent about what's working and what's not. I also remember what my manager taught me when I went to Little Rock for my first job. She said, 'Whether they're in the office or in the factory, they're all still people. Get to know your people.'"

When asked about what role mentoring played in his career, Adam said, "Mentoring is the foundation of it all. I had a great mentor at Caterpillar and at McDonald's. It really saves time on the learning curve. It's good to have someone you can bounce ideas off of, and politics do play a role. You have to figure out when to fall on the sword and when to give the VP the lollipop they want."

TEACH ME HOW TO CREATE A STRATEGIC BUSINESS CASE FOR MY NEW IDEAS

After your employee has developed a proof of concept that you agree is worth pursuing, the next step is helping them create a strategic business case to "sell" their idea because in the end, their success revolves around the involvement of others. Whether they're asking for funding or staffing or someone's participation to accomplish their idea, helping them build a business case is a valuable skill and a critical part of the "ask."

Teaching employees the value of gaining buy-in from others, knowing who is pivotal in the decision making and estimating when the timing is right for the "ask" are all important nuances that can impact a project's success. Admiral William H. McRaven echoes this through in his book, *Make Your Bed*. His premise here is "If you want to change the world, start off by making your bed." As a retired U.S. Navy Seal, he dedicated a chapter in his book to the concept, "You Can't Go It Alone." In the end his counsel is simple: "Never forget your success depends on others." [1]

When employees understand whose support they need and how to appeal to them to move the project forward, then the next questions to ask are: "What's in it for them?" and "How does the success of this project benefit that person or group of people?" If we begin with the end in mind, asking the following questions helps formulate a strategic approach:

- What business problem are we trying to solve?
- What does success look like?
- What's preventing us from achieving this?
- What behaviors or processes need to change for this to be successful?

- How can we drive the desired behavior or process to achieve the desired outcome?

When your employees have answers to these questions, they can formulate the strategy or the "why" behind the "what" they want to accomplish—defining the project's "purpose." Next comes sharing the vision in a way that others see what they see and are inspired to be part of it. Here's an example.

When Neal Lewis came to lead our group at Purina, his reputation preceded him. He was known as a "turn-around guy." He was an expert in taking divisions within the company that were struggling in terms of their profitability, efficiency and employee engagement and "turning them around" to be groups that were profitable, efficient and highly engaged, quickly.

In our case, he had 18 months to turn around the division of about 400 people in 11 different business units or it would be entirely outsourced, and all the jobs would be eliminated. He shared this at the first all-employee meeting and showed us the outsourcing plan, so it was clear that this was a well thought-out and viable leadership option. He went on to show us the collective financials and employee survey scores—both were bad.

Then he continued by saying "This is just where we are today. It's not where we're going to stay. It's where we're going to start. Now, let's see what it looks like on the other side of this journey." And with that, he no longer focused on the negative circumstance or the threat of outsourcing but instead showed us a "vision" of what our improvements were going to look like in 18 months.

He explained that as our group became more efficient and productive, we would become more profitable. As we became more profitable, we would reinvest a certain amount of that profit back into our division. Our offices would be updated. Our systems would be automated so our business units would connect to one another which would change processes but also improve productivity and efficiency.

We would all be cross trained in more than one function so we could develop multiple skills. This would make us more marketable as individuals and would allow us to provide support between business units. This support across business units would allow more flexible schedules, "real time off" where we could disconnect and fewer overtime hours. In a few minutes, we could "see" what our new environment was going to look like and our new culture was going to feel like as we worked together in a different way.

By the end of the meeting, our team was buzzing with excitement, and he closed by saying, "I think we can all see where we want to go and know it's a place we want to be. But I need your help in figuring out the best way to get there. You each are experts in what you do, and I like to talk to the experts. So,

I'll be meeting with each of you individually to get your ideas and learn why you want to succeed and why you want the business to succeed. From where I sit, it looks like we got ourselves an adventure."

The result? Within 18 months, we had restructured the division, automated and streamlined processes and cross trained teams. We were proud of our new surroundings and our newfound efficiency and profitability. The culture had improved tremendously and the good ideas—they just kept coming.

What are our take-aways here? If you want people to buy into change, share the vision. Yes, it's important to show them where they are and explain the current need but painting a clear vision of where you're going, why it's important and what's in it for them propels people toward the vision and helps them "focus forward."

As you work with your employees to develop a business case to sell their idea, ask them to paint that clear picture of where they're heading and why. As they get more proficient at answering the problem-solving questions and painting the vision, you'll begin to see them "pitching" you with a formulated business case, instead of having an "idea" discussion. The challenge I give to my mentees is to formulate a pitch that their boss can answer with a "Yes" or "No." They need to prepare to support the success of the project they believe in. They need to provide enough vision and purpose to be inspirational and enough strategic direction and cost/benefit information to be functional. Here's an example.

As I mentioned in Chapter 1, when I took on the management of building the Caterpillar Visitors Center, the project had been ongoing for eight years, was over budget, over footprint and we hadn't broken ground. As my predecessor retired, he suggested that I ask the Executive Office for more money and ask the city for more land to move forward. He explained that this was the "norm" in building a new facility and that "scope creep" was part of any project and it required more resources. I remember thinking "Heckkkkk no. I'll figure out a different way."

Instead, I focused on reducing the size and cost of the building to work within the original budget and footprint and still achieve our goal of being the first LEED Gold-certified new building for Caterpillar. My goal was to get the project back on track to deliver on time and under budget, so I had some work to do.

I was fortunate to work with an amazing architect who also had an engineering mind and was up for the challenge. As we "value-engineered" the project to reduce cost and footprint, we also questioned the business model. The building was designed to be a training center for employees and a "museum" about Caterpillar, staffed by volunteers and open to the public at no charge. Exhibits were designed to be on the lower level and the main level and upper level were designed to be offices, training rooms and a full industrial kitchen for the staff. The building was shaped in a "V" with the open area in front of the building to display a fountain and a globe structure and the "point" of the "V" was in the back of the lot so there was no "usable" outdoor space.

The architect and I agreed the elaborate entrance was wasted space and expense, as were multiple offices if the staff of docents and tour guides were "on the floor" with guests. We also questioned the industrial kitchen since there was one across the street at the corporate headquarters, and we wondered about all the training rooms. In the eight years this project had been in the works, our Edwards Demonstration facility (where dealers and customers could operate equipment) had expanded to include multiple training rooms, and it was located within miles of the Visitors Center.

If we really didn't need a training center, what did we need? Instead of duplicating capabilities, how could this facility complement the corporate headquarters building across the street and the nearby demonstration and training center? Since our exhibit vendor specialized in "corporate museums," I worked with their team to benchmark other structures and business models to see what made sense for Caterpillar. We looked at Coca-Cola, Purina, Hershey and Deere and learned they generated revenue through admissions, a merchandising store and special events— that often revolved around changing exhibits.

Now, we were on to something. To accommodate our new business model, we "flipped" the building so the entrance was simpler, and the open part of the "V" became usable outdoor space behind the center to host events. We replaced offices with a merchandising store and converted training rooms to all-purpose rooms that could be used for meeting rooms or events. This new structure reduced enough cost and footprint that we delivered on time, under budget and

Photo Credit: Scott Spitznagle, Rock Tail Productions

Photo Credit: Scott Spitznagle, Rock Tail Productions

had a business model that generated revenue and was sustainable.

Many of the things we talked about in this chapter are not new. They're just sequenced in a way that will help your employees expedite their leadership learning curve so they can be a greater support to you more quickly. Whether that means your ability to give them more assignments, share your workload or just spend less time sorting through issues with them, the end result is more productive and more satisfying.

Chapter 10 takes us one step further. As your employees become more independent and self-sufficient, you may also notice areas where you connect and complement. We'll explore this concept next and see if there are even more ways that you can benefit one another.

CHAPTER 10
WHERE DO WE CONNECT AND COMPLEMENT

AS LEADERS, WE ARE ALWAYS LOOKING AHEAD—preparing for what's next. We're planning budget and staffing alternatives for the next upturn or downturn. We're anticipating future customer needs for our products or services. We're developing our team's global capabilities and orchestrating their next moves—all while nurturing a culture that attracts and retains the top talent to lead the next generation.

When it came to preparing for the future at Caterpillar, I remember one leader in particular who simplified the focus for us. When he announced his retirement, he challenged leaders to do two things, "Leave the business better than you found it and in more capable hands." I took his words to heart as I worked with those I led and mentored, always asking myself "Am I preparing them to be more capable by giving them the best of me added to the best of them? Are they better leaders? Are they better problem-solvers? Are they ready to take the business to the next level?"

This focus on the future was grounded in our shared values and purpose as leaders and as a company. The same leader was also fond of saying, "The road to progress begins with a road." His underlying message here was that Caterpillar customers used our equipment to build those roads, and together we were "Making Progress Possible." To us this was more than a tagline or branding at the time, it captured our purpose.

Whether your workforce is local or circles the globe, it likely spans two or three generations. Identifying where leaders and employees of multiple generations connect and complement can be challenging, or it can be unifying. Here are some of the things our young employees are looking for in today's multi-generational, cross-cultural world. These may be good conversation starters in your one-on-one meetings or open discussion topics during your team meetings:

- Identify how our skills and work styles complement each other.
- Remind me why we all matter.
- Spotlight our shared values and purpose.

While these topics naturally mingle within a culture, it's also important to take a look at them individually. In Chapter 6, we delved into why sharing personal and company values is important between a boss and an employee. Now, let's look at the advantages of sharing these things among team members.

IDENTIFY HOW OUR SKILLS AND WORK STYLES COMPLEMENT EACH OTHER

In Chapters 1 and 2, we talked about helping employees identify their transferrable skills and their strengths and shadows. The natural evolution of this individual conversation is having a similar discussion with the entire team to review their collective skills. They might be surprised how talented they are collectively.

Not only can this skills summary create an impressive talent roster, reminding the team of their collective competencies can also serve to buoy them during difficult times. I remember having a team that was struggling to make progress, and when we did this exercise, it was a turning point for them. One team member reviewed the diversity of talent and experience we summarized and was quick to say, "Well, look at us go!" We all got a chuckle out of that recognition moment, and her words soon became the team's "mantra" as they took on and conquered new challenges.

Wes Gray echoed these thoughts when he wrote a recent **Forbes** article entitled, *Why A Multigenerational Workforce Is A Competitive Advantage.* He began by saying, "The wide range of ideas and knowledge from a broad group of people can actually serve the company well and help employees excel in their work." He also cited ways this type of team configuration can promote leadership.

"With so many unique dynamics in a multigenerational workforce, success requires each employee to demonstrate leadership in their role," he said. This leadership manifests itself as employees "lead themselves without supervision, lead peers and lead upward by asking their boss the right questions and not delegating problems upward."[1] These are the "rewards" we talked about in Chapter 9 as employees become more independent and self-sufficient. This also extends the continuity of leadership as employees feel enabled to be a "leader of the moment" in various capacities.

Another benefit of multi-generational teams that Wes cited is the growing trend of "reverse mentoring— a program where a younger employee and an older employee help each other learn new ideas." While younger employees are multi-taskers, tech savvy and proficient with social media, they also are eager to learn and are further engaged when they are mentored by more seasoned employees.

Seasoned employees are often keen to share their knowledge and lessons learned through years of experience. They may view this knowledge sharing as their part of leaving a legacy, which is something that is engaging for them. So, pairing seasoned employees who want to teach with millennials who want to learn can be engaging for both groups and be productive for the team.

Just as different generations possess different skills sets, they also prefer different communication styles. Seasoned employees often prefer face-to-face meetings or phone calls and then emails. Millennials prefer to text or email and would rather join online meetings than attend in person—*even if they're in the same location.* Sometimes alternating the communication medium appeals to teams and other times that just adds a level of frustration, so it's a good discussion topic for the group.

Give Me Encouragement

In Chapter 3 we discussed sincere recognition and referenced the book, *The 5 Languages of Appreciation in the Workplace* by Gary Chapman and Paul White. Their book offers a few thoughts about multigenerational collaboration as well. They suggest that seasoned employees "are fine working in teams to get tasks done, but they have more of a divide-and-conquer approach where they meet together to determine the common goal and then delegate tasks to accomplish individually. Younger employees generally enjoy the process of hanging out together to work cooperatively to achieve the final product."

They also note that recognition preferences may vary as well. Younger employees value words of affirmation first and quality time second—spending time with their leader and taking time off work. Acts of service is a distant third. Seasoned employees also value words of affirmation first, but quality time and acts of service hold about the same value in second place.

One other interesting thought they offer is about the value of hand-written notes of encouragement. They report that for younger employees, "the value of handwritten notes has declined. Rather what *is* important to younger colleagues is the speed with which they receive feedback. Immediate is great. Today is good. Tomorrow is acceptable. After that, you've moved into the realm of history. So, if you want to be effective in communicating that you valued their work on a task, let them know as soon as you can."

A recent Randstad blog entitled, "Pros & Cons of a Multi-generational Workforce" took into account the nuances of today's employees and summarized the collective benefits of multi-generational teams this way. "Companies that can leverage these differences will be able to bring out the best in their people, build a healthy talent pipeline and ensure sustainable business growth."[2]

REMIND ME WHY WE ALL MATTER

Regardless of generation or geography, work styles or recognition preferences, it's important to remind our team members that we all matter, and we each have a role to play in the organization's success.

In Chapter 4, we talked about how leaders look for diverse skillsets, mindsets and experiences as they build teams, and sometimes hiring your "weakness" makes the collective team stronger. We also learned from the words of Neal Lewis who said, "If you were all just alike, I'd only need one of you. I need ALL of you." In her book *Speak,* Sally Lou Oaks Loveman echoed that thought when she said, "If you want your dream to work, your team can't look like you, think like you or act like you. Our differences make us all stronger."[3]

Sometimes our differences are based on the perspective from our individual "comfort zones." Lou Tice in his work with the Pacific Institute defined comfort zones as a place "where the world feels familiar to us."

He went on to say, "We have a lot of comfort zones, depending upon the subject at hand. We have a tendency to think that comfort zones are wonderful because we feel safe. Our comfort zones are based on who we believe we are, and that belief is stored in our subconscious. We make all our decisions, conscious or unconscious, based on that picture of who we believe we are. We look for others who are similar to us, to join us in our comfort zones."

So how can comfort zones impact a team or an organization? "It isn't just individuals who search and find the familiar. Organizations have comfort zones, which leads to stagnation of innovation," he explained. "A lack of diversity of thought and experience causes institutional favoring of the familiar, more commonly known as a blind spot or scotoma. And scotomas cause us to miss options and opportunities."

So why do we all matter? It's our diversity of thought and variety of experiences that lead to innovation, options and opportunities. The key here is to create a space where people feel like their contributions matter and their ideas are valued. As Robert Ingersoll once said, "We all rise by lifting others up."

SPOTLIGHT OUR SHARED VALUES AND PURPOSE

Given the opportunity, people tend to come together when they have shared values and a common purpose. Helping teams focus on their common values and purpose can bring them "back to center" if they've wandered in different directions.

When I worked for the Logistics division of Caterpillar, I saw the value of a shared purpose from the customer's perspective, and it took on a greater meaning for me. Many of our customers were large international corporations—some in the automotive industry. Range Rover was our first automotive customer, and the relationship began on a remote mine site. Because Caterpillar had such an extensive global dealer network, the company was well known for being able to deliver parts anywhere in the world, quickly.

As the story goes, a large Caterpillar mining customer was receiving parts deliveries on its remote mine site daily, and the operator of a Range Rover vehicle was working at the same site and at a standstill, waiting for parts.

After watching the Cat parts delivered day after day to this remote location, the Range Rover operator asked if he could have the parts he needed transported on the Cat trucks so he could get them quickly too. Cat agreed. The Range Rover parts were delivered as promised, and this was the beginning of a new customer relationship and the genesis of new business for Caterpillar. This business further extended our purpose of "Making Progress Possible."

Sharing our Purpose at the Caterpillar Visitors Center

At the Caterpillar Visitors Center we had a unique opportunity to see our purpose in action every day and reinforce it with each other. Our purpose was sharing the world of Caterpillar and its mission of Making Progress Possible with customers, fans and employees from around the world. Our theaters and exhibits featured information about the company's history and products, our unique design and engineering capabilities and the work done every day by our global employees, dealers and customers.

Each morning, we had a team stand-up meeting before we opened the doors, and we reviewed the "run of show" for the day. This included special guests we would be hosting as well as the various groups who would be using our meeting rooms and event spaces. Once we covered the logistics, we always took time for "story telling" and after each story we'd remind ourselves, "And that's why we're here."

Every day, without fail, someone had a new story or recalled one of their favorites about a guest we had welcomed and how Caterpillar in general or their trip to the Visitors Center in particular had made their day or in some cases, impacted their life. Here are a couple of my favorites.

ONE SATURDAY MORNING, a little boy named Max came to visit us. I often talked to the guests as they were anxiously waiting to enter a theater that was the first "attraction." Big kids and little kids were fascinated by this theater that was housed inside a life-size replica of our 797 Mining Truck – the largest of its kind in the world.

The bed of the truck was big enough to house a theater that seated 60 people, and our guests took their seats "in the cab" of the two-story truck, and

This life-size replica of a Caterpillar 797 Mining Truck was one of the featured attractions at the Caterpillar Visitors Center. The bed of the truck housed a 60-seat theater where guests watched a video that took them to job sites around the world to see this machine and others in action.

for about 10 minutes they virtually toured job sites around the world, meeting our customers, watching our equipment work and seeing first-hand the progress that work made possible. The day Max came to visit, we made a different kind of progress possible.

Max's parents brought him to the Visitors Center because he was fascinated with our equipment, not uncommon for a four-year-old boy. What was uncommon was Max's intellect. His parents explained as they purchased their tickets that Max was autistic, and they were working on socialization, being around crowds, having conversations and making eye contact. Since he was so enamored with our equipment, they thought the visit warranted a three-hour drive if it helped him make progress. As we waited for the "movie," Max could hardly contain his excitement. He began reciting facts to me about the 797 truck that would rival the knowledge of most of our docents and some of our engineers.

He knew the size and weight of the truck, the measurements of cab and the tires, its fuel consumption and traveling speed, the load and hauling capacity and how those were impacted by climate, site surface and material. As he continued sharing his knowledge with me, I looked to his parents for approval and then had a seat on the floor next to him—but not too close. We carried on our conversation without making eye contact.

I told Max just how smart I thought he was and he said, "I know." With an encouraging glance from his parents, I continued the conversation and asked him what he wanted to be when he grew up. He said, "An engineer." When I asked what he would like to design, he said, "Big trucks." I told him we hired lots of smart people just like him to be engineers at Caterpillar and asked if he'd like to work at Caterpillar someday.

For the first time since he arrived, he turned his little face and looked directly at me. I knew this was a big step. Then he asked, "Will you be right here?" I said, "Yes Max. I'll be right here." To which he responded, "I'll think about it." His parents smiled, and we were all a little tearful as we ushered Max and the group into the theater. Just as we were ready to make our introductions and start the video, the attending docent leaned my way and whispered, "And that's why we're here." Indeed.

Saturday was usually our busiest day of the week, and the Friday after Thanksgiving was always our biggest day of the year. We saw lots of Caterpillar families who had guests visiting for the holiday and wanted to share the Center with them. We also saw dads and grandpas bringing children and grandchildren that day to keep them entertained while moms shopped. It was without a doubt my favorite day of the year at the Visitors Center—hands down!

ONE OF THOSE Fridays stands out in my mind because it was the day I met Katie. Her grandpa, Bill, was a small-business owner and a good customer of the Visitors Center. He often rented our meeting rooms and held his special events at our facility. He'd mentioned he had a granddaughter he would be bringing to visit the day after Thanksgiving and asked me to set aside time to meet with her to talk about my career, which I was happy to do. I suspected she was a high school or college student thinking about what to study and probably had an interest in communications or event planning, so I thought I was prepared for the discussion.

Boy was I surprised when Bill walked in holding the hand of a little girl who looked to be five or six years old and wasn't even tall enough to see over the ticket counter. As Bill approached the counter, he introduced me to Katie and explained to her that I was the manager of the Caterpillar Visitors Center. Her first question was, "You mean a girl runs this place?" I had to chuckle at her insight, and I said, "Yes. A girl runs this place. A girl built this place, and lots of other girls work at this place."

We took a tour of the building, and I talked to her about managing the build project too and the kinds of things I'd learned. She asked what I did every day and what the other girls did too. Then she asked, "So Caterpillar hires lots of girls?" To which I answered, "Yes. And we're always looking for bright, smart girls just like you to work at Caterpillar when they grow up.

She quickly responded with the question, "How did you know I was smart?

Did my grandpa tell you?" "No," I said. "I can tell by the good questions you asked." By then she'd seen enough and was ready to go into the theater with her grandpa.

They both thanked me for the tour as we parted ways, and I encouraged them to come back and see us again or to call me if Katie had more questions. I wasn't sure if we had planted the seed that Bill was hoping for, but I noticed Katie was unusually quiet as she and her grandpa walked hand in hand toward the theater. Bill asked her what she was thinking about and she said, "I'm thinking about when I get big." He smiled and asked, "What else?" She looked up at him and said one word, "Caterpillar." Bill winked. I nodded and thought to myself, "And that's why we're here."

Closing Thoughts

How is it in your business? Is there something you can all point to and say "And that's why we're here?" Is it easy for your team to spotlight shared values and a shared purpose in the work they do? Is there something they can recognize and reinforce with one another? These are all questions to ask to start a conversation or spur a discussion, but whether it's individual or team focused, it's a discussion worth having.

As we started our journey together, we asked ourselves what we as leaders wanted from millennials. We identified a few things like we wanted to see them engaged and being advocates, demonstrating loyalty for the company. We wanted them to listen to those with experience and consider others' ideas in addition to sharing their own. We wanted them to value learning opportunities, appreciate the investment being made in them and in turn give back to others.

Through the pages we've traveled, we've taken a closer look at both sides of this exchange between leaders and millennials and talked about how to be the best leaders and mentors for them, enabling them to be better team members, engaged employees and future leaders.

Millennials are our future—our future workforce, our future leaders, our future decision makers. Understanding what they want to learn from their boss and see from their company is key to their engagement, their commitment and their loyalty.

If our time together has given you new tools to share, processes to try, or talking points to use as you develop others, then it was time well spent. The employees you're leading right now are your legacy. Through them your own impact is magnified, maybe for years to come. The ideas you've planted with them and the leadership style you've modeled for them will live on as they in turn lead others. Their success and that of future generations is your return on investment. Be proud.

If the servant leader within you is revitalized, and you find yourself asking "What do they need?" and "How can I help them?", you know you're on the right path. And as we close, I'll leave you with one last challenge: I dare you to be the best you can be and help someone else do the same.

After all, that's why we're here.

ABOUT THE AUTHOR

KATHRYN SPITZNAGLE RETIRED FROM CATERPILLAR as the Director of Global Sustainability and founded Mentoring Women Millennials. During her 22 years at Caterpillar, Kathryn held progressive leadership positions including Director of Corporate Communications, Caterpillar Visitors Center Manager, Enterprise Communications Manager, Cat Logistics Global Marketing Manager, Track-Type Tractors Communications and Learning Manager and Marketing Communications Representative.

She was also the project manager for the construction of the Caterpillar Visitors Center, the company's first new building that was LEED Gold certified. The facility welcomed more than 80,000 dealers, customers, employees and Cat fans annually.

Prior to Caterpillar, Kathryn held successive leadership positions in Marketing Communications at Ralston Purina, now Nestlé-Purina, where she learned the value of mentoring, the skill of servant leadership and the privilege of developing others.

Kathryn started her career in magazine publishing and television as a Fashion Editor for SEW NEWS magazine and a script writer for "Make It Fashion," a weekly Lifetime television program. Prior to her work in fashion, Kathryn was an Assistant Editor for Shooting Times magazine and an Editorial Assistant for Rotor & Wing International magazine.

During her career Kathryn has mentored hundreds of young professionals as well as breast cancer survivors and their families. Mentoring is clearly her passion and her purpose.

Kathryn is available for coaching, leader workshop facilitation and inspirational speaking. She also features Rock Star Millennials through her "Rock Star Millennial Spotlight" podcasts. To contact Kathryn, tune in to the podcasts or to nominate a shining example of a Rock Star Millennial in your world, go to Rockstarmillennials.com and click on "contact us."

ACKNOWLEDGMENTS

TO THOSE I MENTOR AND those who mentor me, thank you for your inspiration and your guidance. This book was written to honor and celebrate each of you for the impact you've made in my life and in the lives of so many others.

Thanks to my dear friends and leaders who saw the best in me and cheered me on every step of the way:

Jan Arnold, Lois Boaz, Linda Kraftzenk, Neal Lewis, Jackie McBrady, Lynn Reinacher, Marsha Schoeneman

Thank you to my clients and beta readers for believing in the work I'm doing and the reason it matters. You 've made my business better, my book better and in turn made me better too. Thank you for your investment and your insights:

Rebecca Cartwright, Shelly Erskine, Sam Heer, Steve Klisares, Heidi Kruse, Megan Parsons, Katie Reilly, Anne Schutt, Kelly King Shaw, Diane Shankwitz, Marcy Wiegardt

Thanks to my Rock Star Millennials. You are such a shining example of what your generation is capable of accomplishing, and I'm so proud of each and every one of you! I love your spirit, your creativity and your passion. Don't ever stop improving and making the world a better place, wherever you are:

Lauren Carroll, Adam Hamilton, Amber Kienast, Kelsey Meek, Corrie Heck Scott

Thank you to my editor Bonnie Daneker at Write Along with You. I'm grateful for the Good Lord's Hand that brought us together as NAWBO sisters and partners in this project. Without you I would not have embarked on this book or finished it so quickly. You are my beacon, my muse and my accountability partner.

Most importantly, thank you to my family—my husband Scott, our children Shae and Ian and our daughter-in-law Lauren. My heart is full as I think about the encouragement and support you've provided along this journey.

With love and gratitude,

Kathryn

LEADERSHIP TOOLS

HERE ARE THE LEADERSHIP TOOLS referenced throughout this book for your use. If you'd like them in digital form, go to my website at: ROCKSTARMILLENNIALS.COM

ALIGN YOUR EMPLOYEES' ENERGY WITH SHARED GOALS

EMPLOYEES WANT TO KNOW where they fit in the bigger picture of their department's success and the company's success. After they understand a company's purpose, they want to know how they can contribute to the larger purpose.

This tool helps employees see the alignment between their goals, the department's goals, the company's goals and its larger purpose.

ENTERPRISE PURPOSE:

(Example: Making Progress Possible)

ENTERPRISE GOALS	DEPARTMENT GOALS	PERSONAL GOALS
What goals will deliver success for the enterprise?	What can this department accomplish to support the enterprise goals?	What can I accomplish to support the department goals?
1. *(Example: reduce order-to-delivery time by 25%)*	1. *(Example: reduce transport time)*	1. *(Example: identify additional transportation providers or alternatives)*
2.	2.	2.
3.	3.	3.

DIRECTIONS

- In the header, list the company's purpose.
- In the first column, list the company's top goals.
- In the second column, list the department or work group's top goals in support of the company goals.
- In the third column, ask employees to fill in their goals and explain how their individual work contributes to the success of the department, the company, and the larger purpose.
- Once an employee discovers the value of their work for themselves, ask them to articulate it to you as their leader and to other team members. You'll find they are more engaged and committed to their own success and the company's success.

ROCK STAR MILLENNIALS LEADERSHIP TOOL KIT

BECOMING THE PERSON OF YOUR DESTINY

AS YOU'RE HELPING EMPLOYEES DEFINE the person of their destiny, ask them to answer these questions to create a clear vision of the person they want to become.

1. Who is the person you want to become?

2. Can you visualize that person?

3. What does that person look like... act like?

4. What do people say about that person?

5. What parts of that person are already in place?

6. What parts of that person do you still need to develop?

7. What Does Success Look like For You?

    a) Work

    b) Home

    c) Relationships

8. What steps can you take to become that person?

9. What is one thing holding you back?

10. What is one thing can do today to move forward?

CHARTING YOUR PATH WITH A FROM/TO EXERCISE

FROM *(Describe Current State)*	TO *(Describe Future State)*
1. *(Example: reactive customer service)*	1. *(Proactive customer service)*
2. *(Example: paper-based processes)*	2. *(Digital processes)*
3.	3.
4.	4.
5.	5.
6.	6.
7.	7.
8.	8.

DIRECTIONS

- Ask your team to identify the "From/To" transformation in five or six key areas to create a "picture" of success.
- Summarize the "picture" into a statement that becomes the vision they can articulate.
- Ask the team to define the three or four steps they need to take to get "From" where they are "To" where they want to go in each of the key areas.
- Assemble those steps into an action plan.
- Ask the team to answer the following questions:

    1. **How long will the transformation take?**

    2. **What resources are required?**

    3. **What are the benefits to the business and/or customers?**

- Summarize the resources required and projected benefits in a business case.
- Ask the team to present their vision and business case to leadership.

ROCK STAR MILLENNIALS LEADERSHIP TOOL KIT

CREATING YOUR VISION
WHAT DOES SUCCESS LOOK LIKE?

AS YOU'RE COACHING FUTURE LEADERS, encourage them to define what success looks like. Following are examples of leadership visions or affirmations:

1. When I lead people effectively, they can lead others effectively. It's about touching the lives of people and helping shape their experiences – personally and professionally. What better place to spend my time than unleashing people's talents, skills, ambitions and passions...the things that make them who they are.

2. I enjoy helping others be successful. I want to be a partner in their success.

3. I am who I am both professionally and personally because of leaders who invested in me. This has inspired me to share what I have learned to help others grow.

4. We learn from each other because I have built trusting, lasting relationships with my team members.

5. Employees want to work on my team because of the culture I have created.

6. I am widely known throughout our organization as a leader others model.

CYCLE OF YES

IF YOU HAVE AN EMPLOYEE WHO IS STUCK in the "Cycle of Yes," you can help them break the pattern by teaching them to say "No" graciously. Here are some talking points to share:

- Thank you for thinking of me. I can't help right now, but I wish you all the best with your project.

- It's an honor to be asked. I wish I had the time right now, but I just don't. Thank you for including me.

- I can't take a leadership role right now, but I would be happy to do _____ instead.

- I'm otherwise committed right now, but let me connect you with someone else who might be able to help.

Remind them that choosing to say "No" to something that isn't a priority, means they have more time to say "Yes" to something that is.

ROCK STAR MILLENNIALS LEADERSHIP TOOL KIT

DID IT. DO IT. DONE.

IF YOU HAVE AN EMPLOYEE WHO FEELS THEIR WORK has not been appreciated or they are "reeling" because they helped a co-worker and were not properly thanked, you can stop the negativity and redirect the conversation by asking the following questions:

- When you helped this person was your sole intention to be thanked? Is that why you **DID IT?** (The employee will likely respond that being thanked was not their sole intention.)

- Then why did you **DO IT?** (An employee's typical response is they saw an opportunity and had the skills so they stepped in to help.)

- **DONE.** If your intent was truly to use your skills and help a fellow team member then you did just that. **DONE.**

FOCUS & FINISH

IF YOU HAVE A HIGH-ENERGY EMPLOYEE WHO TENDS to go in multiple directions or gets bored partially through a project and would rather start something new than finish something they started, following are a few tips to help them "Focus & Finish." Begin by helping them define their productivity pattern or profile by asking the following questions:

- Are they more productive when they can work on multiple projects and get energy from the variety of work? Or do they get more accomplished with a linear approach of working on one project through to completion?

- Are they energized by teaming with other people or do they need quiet time to recharge or a combination of both?

- Are they deadline-driven and get a burst of energy to complete the work just prior to the deadline? If so, would setting mini-deadlines in one-hour blocks help?

- If they are working on something creative, are they inspired by music, nature, animals or artwork?

- Does physical activity like walking or stretching help them recharge and re-focus?

The answers to these questions provide a sketch of an employee's productivity profile. Once they define it, they can streamline it and repeat it, moving from focus to finish.

ROCK STAR MILLENNIALS LEADERSHIP TOOL KIT

FROM "STUCK" TO "UNSTUCK"

WHEN AN EMPLOYEE IS "STUCK" and can't seem to move forward on a goal, help them get "unstuck" by reviewing their past successes. If they've completed their "Top 10 List," (also found in this Leadership Tools section) spend some time talking with them about each of those accomplishments and how they feel when they look at that list. Capture some of those emotions. Then ask them how they'll feel when this goal is completed? What does that success look like? The more clearly they can define this vision, the more apt they are to articulate it to others and the further they will be on their way to accomplishing it. Here are the step-by-step discussion topics:

1. Review their past successes.

2. Create a clear vision of what success looks like.

3. Break down the larger goal into smaller steps.

4. Define the individual tasks required to accomplish each step.

5. Assign an owner/vendor and target completion date for each task.

6. Incorporate positive self-talk, affirmations.

7. Identify one task to accomplish today.

GOOD GOSSIP

IF YOU WANT TO TAKE THE CONCEPT OF POSITIVE THINKING beyond the individual and extend it to your entire team to create a culture of positivity, here are a couple of ideas:

- Begin each staff meeting with "Celebrations," recognizing things the team members have learned or accomplished since the last meeting. Take a minute to "revel" with them and watch the tone of the meeting become more positive from the outset.

- Encourage your team to share "Good Gossip" with one another between staff meetings. Good gossip works the same way as bad gossip so we all know how to do it. In its simplest form, ask your employees to find out something positive about someone on the team and tell three people. That's it. Quick. Simple. Positive.

- Introduce the "Tell me something good" game. It's easy to play and uplifting. Each team member commits to having a positive thought, saying, or humorous story in mind at all times. Whenever another team member needs a boost, they can reach out to a peer with the request "tell me something good" and the team member responds with their positive thought or story, no questions asked. This gives employees a safe way to ask for encouragement when they need it without any further explanation about what might be troubling them.

- End each staff meeting with the question, "What are you looking forward to?" This ends the meeting on a high note and gets the team focusing forward—positively!

ROCK STAR MILLENNIALS LEADERSHIP TOOL KIT

HEALTHY PATH

WHEN YOU HAVE AN EMPLOYEE WHO IS NOT PROGRESSING and seems to be inwardly focused, use the following line of questions to redirect them on a healthy path. Helping someone else gets the focus off them and generates some positive energy that powers action.

1. What problem are we trying to solve?

2. What steps do you need to take to get from here to there?

3. What can you impact?

4. What's one thing you can do today to move forward?

5. How long will it take to do that one thing?

6. Before you do that one thing today, help someone else—right now. Reach out to encourage, support or help one person.

7. This simple act of kindness will make them feel better, make you feel better and give you energy to accomplish your one task.

8. Let me know when you've done it and we'll celebrate.

ROCK STAR MILLENNIALS LEADERSHIP TOOL KIT

HERO PAGE

THE "HERO" PAGE IS A PLACE TO RECORD GOOD THINGS about a leader, team member or coworker. List the things you know/learn about them (names of a spouse or significant other, children, pets, favorite foods, hobbies, etc.), gifts or talents you've observed as well as things you respect and admire about them.

WHY IS THIS IMPORTANT?

1. Having a place to record these positives will encourage you to look for them.

2. At some point, you'll have a tough day with this person and reviewing these notes will provide perspective and remind you of all the good you've seen in that person.

3. Some time they will have a bad day and the positive thoughts you've recorded here are ones you can pass along to them at just the right moment... lifting their spirits... and yours.

Name:

Three things I have learned:

1.

2.

3.

Gifts and talents I have observed:

•

•

•

What I respect and admire:

•

•

•

ROCK STAR MILLENNIALS LEADERSHIP TOOL KIT

JUST THE FACTS — HONEST EVALUATIONS

IF YOU HAVE AN EMPLOYEE WHO HAS AN INFLATED OPINION of their accomplishments or is pressing for a higher merit rating or compensation than you feel they've earned relative to their goals or peers, start the conversation by accepting their premise and asking the following questions to gather facts:

- As the top contributor, have you met all your goals?

- Have you exceeded any goals? If so, how?

- In what ways have you contributed to the success of others?

- Where have you demonstrated creativity or innovation to improve a product, process or service?

- What have you done beyond your personal goals to help advance the enterprise or the business as a whole?

These are good conversation starters and can help an employee quantify his or her achievements and focus beyond themselves to help others and the business succeed.

ROCK STAR MILLENNIALS LEADERSHIP TOOL KIT

MENTOR/MENTEE DISCUSSION TOPICS

1. **GETTING TO KNOW YOU:** Tell me about you personally—your family, your personal favorites (food, activities, books, music, shows, travel) what do you like to do outside of work, describe your best boss, best day at work, worst day at work, what would have made worst day better?

2. **RECOGNITION:** How do you like to be recognized and what's the best way to demonstrate "genuine concern" for you? Review "5 Languages of Appreciation in the Workplace."

3. **VISION AND VALUES:** Define what you want out of this job, what excites you about it, and how it fits with your career vision and values.

4. **SUCCESS:** Why do you want to succeed? Why do you want this company/organization to succeed?

5. **REVITALIZE:** Identify three things that revitalize you and ways to bring some portion of that to work.

6. **SELF TALK:** You can track it & improve it—about yourself and others—and discover why it's critical.

7. **VISUALIZATION:** Imagine the situation you want. Use positive affirmations to move toward it.

8. **TIMING AND THRESHOLDS:** How many hours a week are you working? What are the five to six primary things you do at work consistently? What is the best time of day for you to do these tasks? What is your threshold for each? How can you intentionally build energy into your day?

9. **MANAGING EXPECTATIONS:** Learn how to track others' behavior patterns, get ahead of the pattern of behavior and find the positive in each person.

10. **SEPARATING ISSUES FROM EMOTIONS:** Learn how to stop "the reeling", determine what you can impact, keep perspective.

11. **HERO/STAR PAGES:** Create a "Hero" page for your boss and "Star" pages for your team, record things you've learned about them, respect/admire about them and document the good things they've done.

12. **GOOD GOSSIP:** Make a practice of catching someone doing something good, recognize the individual and tell three people.

13. **SERVANT LEADERSHIP:** Lead by serving others... discover how serving others also serves you.

14. **CREATING YOUR DESTINY:** Define the person you want to become and the life you want to lead ...then live intentionally each day along the way.

ROCK STAR MILLENNIALS LEADERSHIP TOOL KIT

POSITIVE SELF-TALK & AFFIRMATIONS

ASK EMPLOYEES TO TRACK THEIR NEGATIVE SELF-TALK and write a positive self-talk statement they can use instead as they transform their inner dialog from a negative conversation to a positive one. An affirmation captures a future state in the present tense, as if it's true today.

NEGATIVE SELF-TALK	POSITIVE SELF-TALK
1. (Example: I'm not qualified to interview for this job.)	1. (I have most of the qualifications for this job and I can learn the rest.)
2. (Example: I'm an imposter. I shouldn't be speaking.)	2. (I have expertise and I'm here to share it with others.)
3.	3.
4.	4.
5.	5.
6.	6.
7.	7.
8.	8.
9.	9.
10.	10.

ROLE PLAY OR DRY RUN

ROLE PLAY

WHEN AN EMPLOYEE IS PREPARING FOR A DIFFICULT CONVERSATION with a client, peer or another leader, practicing the conversation with them through role playing can be helpful. You can support them by:

- Rehearsing the discussion from greeting to closing

- Playing the role of the peer, client or leader

- Asking tough questions or offering "push back"

- Behaving like the client

- After each practice session, provide positive feedback and areas for improvement

DRY RUN

WHEN AN EMPLOYEE IS PREPARING TO GIVE A PRESENTATION to leaders, peers, or clients, allowing time to practice is key. The practice or "dry run" should include:

- Speaking out loud

- Repeating the key messages multiple times until there is a natural flow

- Standing in the front of the room or on the stage, preferably in the room where they will present

- Practicing with the microphone, remote and any other technology

- Timing the presentation delivery each time to build consistency

- Preparing answers for probable questions from the audience

ROCK STAR MILLENNIALS LEADERSHIP TOOL KIT

SEPARATING ISSUES FROM EMOTIONS

SHARE THE FOLLOWING WITH EMPLOYEES to help them stop the "reeling."

1. **Take out a blank piece of paper and draw a big + sign, dividing the paper into four quadrants** *(see next page)*.

   - Label the upper left box ISSUES (from the situation/conversation)
   - Label the upper right box EMOTIONS (underlying messages from the situation/conversation)
   - Label the lower right box EMOTIONS (I feel now)
   - Label the lower left box ISSUES (I can impact)

2. **Start at the upper left box and list out the ISSUES of the situation/conversation. These are the issues that were discussed like: performance, client issues, projects, job requirements, budget planning, etc.**

3. **Then move to the upper right-hand box and jot down EMOTIONS of the discussion.**

   - These are quotes/words that were said to you by someone
   - They are the comments that keep ringing in your head
   - Also note any undertones that weren't actually said but may have been implied or apparent in body language or tone.

4. **In the lower right-hand box, list EMOTIONS I feel now.**

   - Mad, hurt, confused, overwhelmed, inadequate
   - Be honest and list each one
   - Take your time.

5. **Move on to the lower left-hand box and list ISSUES I can impact**

   - List things you can do... those within your control.
   - These might be things like... collect information about the situation... or plan a training session with someone who has experience... or talk to someone who made this work successfully and discover what steps they took.
   - Another important thing to do is help someone else... right now, do something positive for someone else. Helping is part of healing... and it helps to redirect some positive energy, even if it's a quick text or call.

...continued on next page

ROCK STAR MILLENNIALS LEADERSHIP TOOL KIT

6. **Now you've started to develop an action plan...one you can impact. You've stopped the "reeling." You're focused on finding a solution. You're back in control. You decide next steps but before you take any action, let's put this in perspective.**

- Where does this situation fit in the magnitude of life? Is this situation life threatening to you... your spouse... friends... family?

- Does this situation have ramifications for the rest of your life? Is it irreversible? My guess is this situation is about a job... actually about one small piece of a job... on one day... at one moment... a job that you'll have for a relatively short time... a few months or years... which is one piece of your career... which is one piece of your life.

- Given that perspective, don't trade one more minute of your life reeling about this issue. Start by doing one thing right now to help or encourage someone else and then get on with your action plan. Get on with your day.

1. Issues (WHAT was the situation or conversation?)	2. Emotions (WHAT was the underlying message?)
4. Issues (WHAT can you impact?)	**3. Emotions (WHAT emotions do you feel?)**

ROCK STAR MILLENNIALS LEADERSHIP TOOL KIT

SET THEM UP TO SUCCEED—CLEAR EXPECTATIONS

ONE OF THE MOST IMPORTANT THINGS YOU CAN PROVIDE to a new employee or an employee coming into a new role is clear expectations. In short, employees want to know:

- What do you want me to do?

- How will you evaluate and compensate me?

A few basic steps that provide answers to these questions are:

- Review a job description (beyond the job posting) with specifics about the responsibilities and deliverables.

- Provide standard work or defined processes for the basic tasks required.

- Supply a Frequently Asked Questions (FAQ) document or interactive site for basic product and process information.

- Offer training in a variety of mediums for different types of learners, including oral, audio, visual and hands-on or job shadowing.

- Set three to five goals with a measurable outcome, timeline and definition of success.

Explain the compensation or reward structure for the particular role and provide examples, especially if bonuses are based on a number of deliverables.

STOP. START. CONTINUE.

THIS IS ANOTHER EXERCISE to do with your team in times of change. Simply ask the questions:

- What should we **START** doing?

- What should we **STOP** doing?

- What should we **CONTINUE** doing?

They may have innovative ideas for things the team should **START** doing and could be worth exploring. Be sure to ask for the "why" behind each suggestion to better understand the motivation or logic.

The tasks they identify to **STOP** doing may be things that are outdated, no longer add value, or they don't understand the purpose of the work. If the purpose is in question and the task has a value, take the time to communicate its larger purpose to employees.

As you discuss things to **CONTINUE** doing, use the opportunity to ask for improvement ideas. Is there a way to do something better, faster, cheaper? All are good topics for discussion at a time of change.

TALKING POINTS FOR TOUGH CONVERSATIONS

WHEN YOU'RE PREPARING FOR A TOUGH CONVERSATION with an employee, having well-planned, organized talking points is key. Following are some talking points or framing statements to use for redirecting employees:

- "We both want the same thing and that's for you to be successful. Now, let's figure out the next steps to get you there."

- "When I look at the skills you've demonstrated, I've seen _____, _____ and _____. The skills gap I see is _____. Let's get focused on closing that gap because _____ is a skill you'll need to advance."

- As you progress in your career, this is one thing that can hold you back so let's fix it."

- "The leadership I'm looking for from you is_____."

- I see you as a future leader and this is a skill you need to develop to get there.

- As we're building up your skillset for leadership, there's one area where we need to focus more energy going forward and that's _____."

3-BUCKET EXERCISE (WEEKLY MEETING FORMAT)

ASK EMPLOYEES TO TAKE TWO MINUTES EACH DAY to track work and non-work celebrations and stresses—just quick notes in their phone or notebook, nothing fancy. Categorize the notes in three "buckets."

(Celebrations—things I learned/mastered)   *(Things I'm aware of and need to learn more about or master)*   *(Things I don't understand, didn't realize were part of the position or part of life and seem overwhelming)*

During your regular meetings, you will be their accountability partner. You'll review what's going on in their world and celebrate their progress.

HERE ARE SOME TALKING POINTS FOR YOU TO USE WITH EMPLOYEES:

- Tracking what you mastered each day/week provides a sense of accomplishment and helps you realize you are making quantifiable progress. It also gives you pause to celebrate and builds confidence. You'll soon realize if you mastered those things, you can master whatever is next.

- When you identify the issues you're aware of but haven't yet resolved we'll work together to put an action plan in place, break it down into smaller steps that you can accomplish and develop a repeatable process that works for you to meet your goals—every time.

- Talking about the things that are overwhelming or frustrating is just plain healthy and honest. You'll learn how to "fess it and fix it," separate issues from emotions, reduce your stress, identify what you can impact and move forward from "stuck" to "success."

- Together...there's nothing we can't figure out, and it's so fun to watch the things in your third bucket one week move to bucket number two as we develop a plan... and then move to bucket number one... and pretty soon, you have a list of remarkable accomplishments... and lots to be proud of too.

- We'll spend time working on short-term goals and create long-term leadership development goals as we define the "Person of Your Destiny" ...what does that person look like? Act like? What has that person accomplished? How do they lead? What do people say about that person? We'll identify the pieces of that person that are there and the pieces you want to develop. Then we'll create an action plan and goals to move you closer to that leader you'll soon become.

- Let's get started!

ROCK STAR MILLENNIALS LEADERSHIP TOOL KIT

3 THINGS THAT REVITALIZE

HERE'S THE WAY TO BRING THIS INTO YOUR LEADERSHIP STYLE and a way to communicate it to your millennial team members. It's really a simple four-step process.

1. The first step is being aware of the need to revitalize.

2. The second step is identifying what you like to do and understanding which three things truly revitalize you.

3. The third step is allotting time to do those things that rejuvenate you and making them a priority.

4. The last step is incorporating rejuvenation into your daily work life and doing it intentionally as a part of self-care and leadership.

NOTE: *When you have an employee who is looking ahead to a particularly stressful week, work with them to schedule additional time to rejuvenate or help them prioritize the most impactful rejuvenation for the least amount of time commitment, like one-minute meditation.*

ROCK STAR MILLENNIALS LEADERSHIP TOOL KIT

TIMING & THRESHOLDS

UNDERSTANDING TIMING AND THRESHOLDS allows you to set up each day for success by controlling what you can, organizing and prioritizing key processes and people. By understanding your natural working rhythm, you can visualize and create your ideal day.

STEP 1: IDENTIFY

List the tasks you regularly do on the job (emails, phone calls, meetings, writing, etc.) and estimate how much time you spend on each per day:

_____ Time: _____

_____ Time: _____

_____ Time: _____

_____ Time: _____

_____ Time: _____

_____ Time: _____

_____ Time: _____

_____ Time: _____

_____ Time: _____

_____ Time: _____

...continued on next page

ROCK STAR MILLENNIALS LEADERSHIP TOOL KIT

Which activities ENERGIZE YOU?	Which activities DRAIN YOU?
What is the best time of day to do those activities that ENERGIZE YOU?	What is the best time of day to do those activities that DRAIN YOU?
Who ENERGIZES YOU?	Who DRAINS YOU?
What is the best time of day to see/meet with those who ENERGIZE you?	What is the best time of day to see/meet with those who DRAIN you?

...continued on next page

ROCK STAR MILLENNIALS LEADERSHIP TOOL KIT

STEP 2: PRIORITIZE

Consider how you assign value to a task or a relationship/person. (i.e.: urgent/ important/not urgent/ not important; deadlines, etc.). Rank your activities in order of importance.

1. _____

2. _____

3. _____

4. _____

5. _____

6. _____

7. _____

8. _____

STEP 3: ORGANIZE

Consider how to reduce steps and lump "like tasks" together to improve efficiency. Now, organize your activities into the following buckets: what tasks can you automate, which can you delegate and what can you stop doing to set your day up for success?

AUTOMATE (Create templates/standard work or tasks you can simplify)	DELEGATE (Tasks you can assign to others)	STOP DOING (Tasks that are non-value added and consume too much time in relation to the return on investment)

ROCK STAR MILLENNIALS LEADERSHIP TOOL KIT

TOP 10 LIST

ASK YOUR EMPLOYEES TO CREATE their own "Top 10 List" by listing their top successes, accomplishments, or tough things they've overcome.

1. _____

2. _____

3. _____

4. _____

5. _____

6. _____

7. _____

8. _____

9. _____

10. _____

Once they've completed the list, ask them how they feel. Proud? Successful? Grateful? Whatever the feeling, ask them to take minute to relish it.

As they face tough challenges going forward, remind them of this list and assure them that the person who accomplished these things can surely tackle whatever comes next.

TRACKING BEHAVIOR PATTERNS TO BRING OUT THE BEST IN ALL OF US

AS LEADERS WE KNOW THERE'S A PEARL inside each one of us ...and each one of our team members, peers, leaders and customers. Sometimes our job is to help employees look past another person's tough shell and "sticky inside" to find the pearl. If an employee is consistently having difficulty with a certain individual, tracking the behavior patterns of that person may help them with future interactions. Here's how:

1. As your employee prepares for a meeting with the difficult individual, ask your employee to make a cheat sheet. Ask them to use a sticky note and list a few positive and negative behaviors they've seen in the past—things they might expect to see again. *(Positives could be good eye contact, warm welcome, open dialog about the account/team, etc. Negatives could be the client jumping to conclusions without all the facts, giving incomplete information, blaming, yelling, fit throwing, etc.)*

2. During the meeting, as your employee sees each behavior demonstrated, ask them to place a checkmark next to it, making one checkmark for every time they see the behavior. This tactic has a wonderful calming effect during the meeting. It transforms your employee from a recipient into a spectator. Instead of taking these things personally, they're simply observing behavior... and making a few checkmarks while they take meeting notes... and smile to themself about how calm they are today compared to prior meetings.

3. After the meeting, ask them to look at their marks. They may find there are more positives than they realized—build on those. They may also find they can translate accusations into needs by asking "What was at the root of this comment? What do they really need? How can I help them?"

    • They may find the negatives come in a pattern of behavior. Ask them to keep tracking the behavior in future calls and meetings. Remember, three instances of a behavior constitutes a pattern. Once they see the pattern, they can predict it. Once they can predict it, they can plan to avoid it, get ahead of it and/or respond to it.

    • In the end, your employee can't control how people have acted in the past, but they can control how they re-act... and pro-act... to change someone's behavior in the future. All the sudden, finding a pearl... sounds like an adventure!

 ROCK STAR MILLENNIALS LEADERSHIP TOOL KIT

WHAT I MISS & WHAT I WOULD HAVE MISSED

AS EMPLOYEES START A NEW JOB OR EXPERIENCE A CHANGE in leadership or environment, ask them to list things they miss about the former job/leader and list what they would have missed if they hadn't made the change. This exercise typically eases the change, provides perspective, and positions employees to focus forward with positivity.

WHAT I MISS *(from the situation before the change)*	WHAT I WOULD HAVE MISSED *(if I hadn't made the change)*
1.	1.
2.	2.
3.	3.
4.	4.
5.	5.
6.	6.
7.	7.
8.	8.
9.	9.
10.	10.
11.	11.

ROCK STAR MILLENNIALS LEADERSHIP TOOL KIT

ENDNOTES

CHAPTER 3

1. Rosenbluth, Hal, and Diane McFerrin Peters. "The Customer Comes Second."

2. Danforth, William H. "I DARE YOU."

3. Chapman, Gary, and Paul White. "The 5 Languages of Appreciation in the Workplace."

CHAPTER 5

1. Wade, Sophie. "The Six Secrets of Effective Remote Working and Collaborating." https://www.huffpost.com/entry/the-six-secrets-of-effective-remote-working-and-collaborating_b_5a3806dde4b02bd1c8c60904.

2. Wade, Sophie. "Productivity And Performance With A Distributed Workforce: Control, Choice, And Communication." https://www.huffpost.com/entry/productivity-and-performance-with-a-distributed-workforce_b_57d3215de4b0f831f7071cb6.

CHAPTER 6

1. "The Deloitte Global Millennial Survey 2019." https://www2.deloitte.com/content/dam/Deloitte/global/Documents/About-Deloitte/deloitte-2019-millennial-survey.pdf

2. Tuff, Chris. "The Millennial Whisperer." New York: Morgan James Publishing, 2019.

3. Despain, Jim, and Jane Bodman Converse. "...And Dignity for All."

CHAPTER 7

1. Tice, Lou. "Smart Talk for Achieving Your Potential."

2. Loveman, Sally Lou Oaks. "Speak."

3. Roedl, Thomas, Dr. "Effectiveness and Efficiency—the Secret Ingredients of Productivity" https://www.paperlessmovement.com/blog/effectiveness-and-efficiency-the-secret-ingredients-of-productivity/

4. Cohen, Jennifer. "Busy vs. Productive: Which One Are You?" https://www.forbes.com/sites/jennifercohen/2018/06/25/busy-vs-productive-which-one-are-you/#33d991c47d79

CHAPTER 8

1. Taylor, William. "Simply Brilliant: How Great Organizations Do Ordinary Things in Extraordinary Ways."

2. Wambach, Abby "Wolfpack."

CHAPTER 9

1. McRaven, William H., Admiral. "Make Your Bed."

CHAPTER 10

1. Gray, Wes. "Why A Multigenerational Workforce Is A Competitive Advantage." https://www.forbes.com/sites/wesgay/2017/10/20/multigeneration-workforce/#1c4c4c2d4bfd

2. "Pros & Cons of a Multi-Generational Workforce." https://www.randstad.com.hk/workforce-insights/workforce-trends/pros-and-cons-of-a-multi-generational-workforce/

3. Loveman, Sally Lou Oaks. "Speak."

BIBLIOGRAPHY

- Chapman, Gary, and Paul White. "The 5 Languages of Appreciation in the Workplace." Chicago: Northfield Publishing, 2019.

- Cohen, Jennifer. "Busy vs. Productive: Which One Are You?" Forbes, June 25,2018. https://www.forbes.com/sites/jennifercohen/2018/06/25/busy-vs-productive-which-one-are-you/#33d991c47d79

- Danforth, William H. "I DARE YOU." St. Louis, MO: Privately Published, 1954.

- Despain, Jim, and Jane Bodman Converse. "...And Dignity for All." New Jersey: Publishing as Financial Times Prentice Hall, 2003.

- "The Deloitte Global Millennial Survey 2019." https://www2.deloitte.com/content/dam/Deloitte/global/Documents/About-Deloitte/deloitte-2019-millennial-survey.pdf

- Gray, Wes. "Why A Multigenerational Workforce Is A Competitive Advantage." Forbes, October 20, 2017. https://www.forbes.com/sites/wesgay/2017/10/20/multigeneration-workforce/#1c4c4c2d4bfd

- Loveman, Sally Lou Oaks. "Speak." Bloomington, IN: Balboa Press, 2019.

- McRaven, William H., Admiral. "Make Your Bed." New York: Grand Central Publishing, 2017.

- "Pros & Cons of a Multi-Generational Workforce." Randstad blog, 2019. https://www.randstad.com.hk/workforce-insights/workforce-trends/pros-and-cons-of-a-multi-generational-workforce/

- Roedl, Thomas, Dr. "Effectiveness and Efficiency—the Secret Ingredients of Productivity," paperless movement.com, February 8, 2020. https://www.paperlessmovement.com/blog/effectiveness-and-efficiency-the-secret-ingredients-of-productivity/

- Rosenbluth, Hal, and Diane McFerrin Peters. "The Customer Comes Second." New York: Harper Collins, 2002.

- Taylor, William. "Simply Brilliant: How Great Organizations Do Ordinary Things in Extraordinary Ways." New York: Penguin Random House, 2016.

- Tice, Lou. "Smart Talk for Achieving Your Potential." Seattle: Pacific Institute Publishing, 1995.

- Tuff, Chris. "The Millennial Whisperer." New York: Morgan James Publishing, 2019.

- Wade, Sophie. "The Six Secrets of Effective Remote Working and Collaborating," HUFF POST, December 18, 2017. https://www.huffpost.com/entry/the-six-secrets-of-effective-remote-working-and-collaborating_b_5a3806dde4b02bd1c8c60904

- Wade, Sophie. "Productivity And Performance With A Distributed Workforce: Control, Choice, And Communication," HUFF POST, September 9, 2016. https://www.huffpost.com/entry/productivity-and-performance-with-a-distributed-workforce_b_57d3215de4b0f831f7071cb6

- Wambach, Abby "Wolfpack." New York: Celadon Books, 2019.

INDEX

T

V

W

CPSIA information can be obtained
at www.ICGtesting.com
Printed in the USA
LVHW050930200221
679498LV00043B/527